SIBELIUS
and his world

SIBELIUS
and his world

BY ROBERT LAYTON

THAMES AND HUDSON · LONDON

Copyright © 1970 Thames and Hudson Ltd

The publishers acknowledge their use of
Jean Sibelius – Kuvaelämäkerta by Ilkka Oramo
Copyright © 1965 Kustannusosakeyhtiö Otava, Helsinki, Finland
from which the illustrations appearing in this
volume have been reproduced

Printed in Finland

500 13026 4

AT THE TIME of Sibelius's birth, the mid-1860s, Finland was no more than an outpost of the Tsarist empire. Russia herself was backward, and the Crimean war and the abolition of serfdom were very recent history. Finland was only slowly awakening to her own sense of identity. The Finnish language occupied a slender place in the cultural life of the country, and affairs of state were still conducted in Swedish. When the Russians took over Finland at the beginning of the nineteenth century, they chose to rule the country through the existing administrative apparatus: the Swedish civil service which had run the country during the five hundred years of Swedish hegemony. For the greater part of the century the country enjoyed a fair measure of autonomy, and it was not until the 1890s, when the movement for national self-determination began to gather momentum, that the Tsarist government tightened its control over the country and introduced repressive legislation.

Jean Sibelius was born on 8 December 1865, in a small garrison town called Tavastehus in Swedish, Hämeenlinna in Finnish. It lies in the southern and central part of Finland, and Sibelius's father practised as a doctor to the Russian soldiery stationed there. Like most members of the professional middle classes, the Sibelius's were Swedish-speaking; the town was predominantly middle-class, and so Sibelius had little contact with Finnish during his early childhood. He could have had little recollection of his father, who died when he was only two. The elder Sibelius appears to have been well-liked in Hämeenlinna and conscientious; he succumbed to the typhoid epidemic that assailed both garrison and town in 1868. Sibelius's upbringing, then, was left to his mother and a number of female relatives.

At first sight, Hämeenlinna might seem to provide an unpromising *Childhood* milieu for the childhood of a great composer. True, it was no musical or cultural centre of consequence, but then neither was Helsinki itself. The capital did not have a permanent symphony orchestra until the

1880s, when Robert Kajanus founded the Helsinki City Orchestra (Helsingfors Stadsorkester), and the Finnish national opera was not put on a solid basis until 1912, when the soprano Aino Ackté, for whom Sibelius composed *Luonnotar,* founded the opera house in conjunction with the firm of Fazer. Such musical stimulus as Sibelius had came from amateur sources: the family made music in the home with their friends and relatives; his brother played the cello and his sister was a pianist.

But in early childhood the important thing is the development of secure human foundations, rather than the presence of any specific stimulus, and Sibelius's childhood seems to have been a happy and contented one. He must have felt the lack of a father, but he seems to have had the wide interests and the appetites of any normal, healthy child. His oldest childhood friend, Walter von Konow, has testified to his imagination, his liveliness and sense of fun, his love of play-acting – he and his friends often acted out the stories of Hans Andersen or Topelius, or even plots that the boy himself had invented. Like most children, he was capable of sudden switches of feeling, from the gayest abandon to

6

2　The young Sibelius

the deepest melancholy. If the domestic atmosphere at Hämeenlinna, his winter home, was harmonious, his happiness in the summer months, spent at Loviisa with a doting grandmother and aunt, was unbounded. Those who have experienced the white nights, the intensity and stillness of the northern summer, the pallor and delicacy of the colouring, will have some idea of the intoxicating effect of these summer months as well as the gentle melancholy their transience induces. Love of nature is a characteristic of most Scandinavian peoples, and Sibelius's childhood gave him ample opportunity to nourish his love of the Finnish country-side, a feeling that was one of the motivating forces in his art and a dominant feature of his personality.

When he was eleven, his mother took what was to prove a very important step: she enrolled him at the Hämeenlinna Suomalainen Normaalilyseo, the Finnish-speaking grammar school of the town. It is a measure of the scant regard in which the Finnish language was held that there were no important centres of higher education that used the vernacular as the medium of teaching. Practically all teaching in Finnish

3 Hämeenlinna, an engraving by C. Jansson, 1867

grammar schools was conducted in Swedish. The Hämeenlinna Suomalainen Normaalilyseo was a pioneering school in this respect, and it was
a far-sighted decision on his mother's part to bring him into so early a
contact with the Finnish language. It opened his eyes to another source
of inspiration, apart from nature, that was to be a vital force in his
musical personality: namely Finnish mythology as enshrined in the
national epic, the *Kalevala*. The *Kalevala* had made its appearance in
1835 and was something of a sensation. Its rhythm was to be imitated
a couple of decades later by Longfellow in *Hiawatha,* though the pattern
is uniquely suited to the dark Finnish legends and has none of the faintly
ludicrous overtones of the same rhythm in English. Elias Lönnrot col-
lected a vast amount of folk literature during the 1830s and 1840s, including the *Kantele* and *Kanteletar,* and its impact on Sibelius was as
great as that of the nature poetry of Runeberg and Rydberg. Both were
a constant source of inspiration: the *Kalevala* he drew on for works as
far apart in time as the 'Kullervo' Symphony (written at the outset of
his career), *Pohjola's Daughter* (1906) and *Luonnotar* (1913), the strangest
and most elusive of his tone-poems, while he chose a Runeberg poem
almost as his first vocal setting and sustained an interest in the great poet
until the end of his career.

Academically, Janne, as he was called in childhood, was not in any
sense remarkable; when his interests were not engaged, he was some-

8

4 Sibelius's parents ▶

thing of a day-dreamer and had a tendency to be restless in class. However, he showed a healthy intellectual curiosity in those things that aroused an initial response in him, and it was the arts rather than any scientific discipline that he warmed to. What, then, of his early musical impressions? The keyboard did not seem to attract him; he began lessons when he was nine, but he never really developed much feeling for the piano, even in his maturity. The finest of his piano pieces, such as the Sonatinas, op. 67, are effective enough despite their limited range of musical devices; but, for the most part, his piano-writing is neither idiomatic nor instinctive. The violin, however, was another matter: for this he had great natural feeling, as is shown by such works as the Humoresques for violin and orchestra and the better-known Violin Concerto. He embarked on serious study of the violin too late to make a career as a virtuoso, his first ambition, and, although he gained considerable prowess as a player, had to abandon this idea when he came to study music in earnest.

Student years He began his studies with Gustav Levander, Hämeenlinna's leading musician, who was in charge of music at the garrison. But he had already begun composing before he went to Levander: his first surviving piece dates from his tenth year and is called *Vattendroppar (Drops of Water)*. It is scored for violin and cello pizzicato, and on the same piece of manuscript paper there is a short sketch for string quartet. His activities as a composer, like his knowledge of the repertoire, were circumscribed by what he could hear played at home or what he and his friends could play themselves. There are chamber works dating from his teens for various combinations, including a quartet for the somewhat unlikely combination of violin, cello, harmonium and piano. The harmonium part was apparently intended for Fru Evalina Sucksdorff, Sibelius's great-aunt, the cello part for her husband or possibly Sibelius's brother, the piano probably for one of his aunts, while the violinist was the composer himself. Such were the modest but practical inspirations for composition. John Rosas, the Finnish authority on these early years, suggests (rightly, I think) that this quartet was composed while Sibelius was still at school.

He wrote many other works during these years, for more orthodox ensembles. Indeed, his output of chamber music is a good deal larger than most people imagine. In 1887, when he was twenty-one, he spent the summer at Korpo, playing chamber music with his brother Christian and with Fru Ina Wilenius. The latter has spoken of his enormous creative energy: he usually composed during the night, and

10

5 Sibelius, aged 2 (on his mother's lap), with his sister Linda

when morning came, a new trio would be ready. These were one-movement pieces, fairly short but often quite difficult to play. It is from this summer that the so-called Korpo Trio dates, and there must have been innumerable similar pieces that no longer survive. The surviving works show three main influences. The first is that of the Viennese classical school, which dominates a good deal of the thematic material and the formal layout of all the larger pieces. Sibelius's feeling for form is discernible even at this early stage. The second is that of the Scandinavian tradition, which at this time chiefly means Grieg and Svendsen. The Violin Sonata in F major, also written in his early twenties, is an instance of this and shows a probable acquaintance with the Grieg sonata in the same key. The debt to the harmonies of Grieg and the Scandinavian tradition, however, is firmly bent to individual ends. Thus, in the songs, Sibelius sheds the influence of Grieg on those albeit rare occasions when he embarks on a Finnish setting, whereas it is much stronger when he sets the Finno-Swedish poets (take the Runeberg settings, for example). The third influence is that of the Russians in general and Tchaikovsky in particular. There are hints of Tchaikovsky in the String Trio in G minor of 1885, but the Russian strain does not become marked until the early 1890s, when Sibelius embarked in earnest on an orchestral canvas.

For all their music-making, Sibelius's family did not take kindly to the idea of his becoming a professional musician, and it was as a law student that he was enrolled at the Tsar Alexander University of Helsinki. The decision seems to have been taken by his grandmother, Fru Borg, though it is only fair to point out that not all the influences in his family were feminine. As a boy, and later as a student, he had a great affection for his uncle Pehr – a man of wide and lively interests, with a passion for astronomy – who lived in Turku (Åbo), the charming seaport some few hours' drive to the west of Helsinki. Sibelius's family, however, made no objection to his enrolling at the School of Music as well, and here he studied violin under Czillag, a Hungarian, and later with Martin Wegelius, the man who, in the 1880s, had founded the School. Wegelius was

◀ 6 Loviisa, where Sibelius spent his summers,
and Hämeenlinna, where he spent the school year

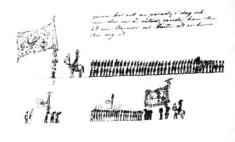

7 A letter from the 8-year-old Sibelius to his aunt and
grandmother, thanking them for their Christmas presents

8 Sibelius's birthplace,
an Empire-style wooden
building in the centre of
Hämeenlinna (next to
the stone-built house),
dating from 1834

perhaps the driving force at this time in Finnish musical life, which had become a good deal livelier during the late 1880s (Liszt's pupil, Sophie Menter, was among the musicians of international repute to visit both Helsinki and Hämeenlinna).

There was no doubt as to where Sibelius's true interests lay. He himself tells a story about an uncle, a teacher from the provinces, who called without warning to see how he was getting on, and found the young man's text-book of Nordic history, part of the prescribed course, open on his desk. Sibelius describes how he had left it aside, hoping for inspiration, and how, exposed month after month to the rays of the sun, the open page had become quite yellow. Finally, the family had to bow to the inevitable, and at the end of the academic year the young man abandoned law for a full-time musical career.

Already his violin-playing had developed so much that he joined the School of Music quartet as second violin, the other members of the group being professors there. In conversation with Karl Ekman, his biographer, Sibelius later recalled that his sole ambition from the age of

14

fifteen onwards was to become a famous violinist, and that he spent the bulk of each day practising to this end. Indeed his early studies of composition were very much a subsidiary activity; it was only when his work with Czillag raised doubts about his capacity to be a virtuoso of the first order, and the creative forces in him gathered strength, that he adjusted himself to the disappointment of abandoning his ambitions. But at least he had had the satisfaction of playing the Mendelssohn concerto, and other virtuoso concertos by Spohr and Kreutzer.

The dominating influence in Sibelius's development was Wegelius, a pupil of Reinecke and Hans Richter. Wegelius was a man of unusual versatility: his experience was wide, he was a composer himself, a pianist and conductor, and had served for some years as a music critic. He was dedicated to his school and inspired an enormous respect in his pupils. He recognized Sibelius's talent and, apart from giving him the requisite grounding in harmony, counterpoint and fugue, took a personal interest in the young man's creative development. Sibelius recounts that he spent many weeks at Wegelius's summer home in the archipelago to the west of Helsinki, where in the mornings he worked at counterpoint, and in the afternoons played sonatas with Wegelius, while the evenings were spent relaxing over a bottle of wine. Wegelius was a man of wide culture, and in the evening they would often discuss or read literary works and books on history. As a keen Wagnerite, he had little time for Brahms – or, for that matter, Tchaikovsky, whom Sibelius admired. When they played Tchaikovsky's enchanting *Sérénade mélancolique*, Wegelius's comment was confined to condemning the 'rubbishy violin part'.

However, he organized his school superbly and attracted to it talent of the first order. In 1888 he engaged none other than Ferruccio Busoni, who was a year younger than Sibelius, and a strong friendship grew up between the two men. In spite of the one being a teacher and the other a pupil, they met daily. Their meetings generally took place at Ericson's café, where Sibelius used to meet his other friends, including Armas Järnefelt and the writer Adolf Paul. On the face of it, there were few common features between the two musicians: the one a former child prodigy, cosmopolitan and brilliant, the other reticent, by comparison provincial, and with a love of nature that Busoni had never had the opportunity to develop. This friendship was an enormous mutual stimulus. Busoni took a keen interest in Sibelius's student works (he played his A minor quartet from sight, so the composer relates), encouraged him at the time of the Suite in A, and championed his work all through his life. He included the Second Symphony in the famous concerts he gave in Berlin at the beginning of the present century and dedicated a movement from his *Geharnischte Suite* to him.

While still a student at the School, Sibelius had quite a success as a composer with two works both produced in his last term, the spring of 1889: a suite in A for string trio, and a quartet in A minor. Karl Flodin, perhaps the most influential of Finnish critics, hailed the latter work in terms of unqualified praise. 'Mr Sibelius has given such striking proof of his original musical talent that one can expect great things of him. In all the different movements

10 Sibelius's first instrument, a harmonium made in Stuttgart

of the Quartet there emerges a fertility of invention and an independence, combined with a mastery of technique, that must be regarded as unique in so young a composer.'

Berlin and Vienna

The impact of Berlin and Vienna on Sibelius was tremendous. This was the first time he had ventured abroad and his first contact with music-making at an international level. Finishing his studies at the School of Music in the spring of 1889, when he was twenty-three, he spent the summer at Loviisa, where he wrote his Quartet in B flat. In the autumn he set out for Berlin, armed with a letter of introduction to Albert Becker, an academic and strict theorist who set the young man to work on Bach and gave him countless exercises in counterpoint and fugue. He ended up, he writes, by knowing the German hymnal back to front and could not help feeling that all those lifeless exercises belonged to the past. Nonetheless, he managed to conceal his boredom, for his real musical education was the concert life of Berlin itself. Here he heard Hans von Bülow give a complete Beethoven sonata cycle, and the Joachim quartet give the late Beethoven quartets. The latter he was hearing for the first time, and his enthusiasm was unbounded. Among contemporary works, he heard Strauss's *Don Juan,* and the sheer orchestral virtuosity of that master, only one year his senior, must have excited his admiration and envy. He had yet to test himself against the orchestra, and his experiences in the concert hall in Berlin certainly provided a strong incentive to do so.

Sibelius took part in quite a lot of chamber music and formed a quartet together with Theodor Spiering, Alf Klingenberg and the German composer Fini Henriques. He saw a good deal of his friend Adolf Paul, who had by now abandoned his ambitions to be a concert pianist and had embarked in earnest on a literary career. With him, Sibelius went to Leipzig the following spring to hear Busoni give Sinding's Piano Quintet with the Brodsky Quartet, and this performance served as a stimulus to the

11, 12 Sibelius's uncle Pehr, from Turku. Below, his other uncle, the sea captain Johan Sibelius

13, 14   Sibelius, aged 11, with his
Hämeenlinna school cap in his hand.
Right, rocks near Loviisa, the kind of
scenery in which he spent his childhood

15 Gustav Levander

16 A picture by Sibelius, drawn on the cover of one of the quartets he played as a student

work on which he himself was engaged, a quintet in G minor. This was the only piece of any substance that Sibelius wrote during his year in Berlin, and he recorded his pleasure at Becker's sympathetic reaction to the work: 'In spite of his orthodoxy on musical questions, Becker showed amazing understanding. I laid my Quintet before him and he examined it with great interest. During the Andante the old man was really moved. He seemed to take great pleasure in the fact that a young man had written something more than just rigid fugues.' To be frank, there is nothing wildly unconventional about the work: the first movement is in sonata form, and three of the other five movements are based on various types of rondo. But the piece does show a growing individuality, considerable confidence in handling the medium and a distinct advance on his earlier works. Wegelius seems to have recognized its merits, for he hastened to introduce two movements from it at a Helsinki concert in May of that year, with Busoni as the pianist and the Norwegian composer Halvorsen leading the quartet.

The most important event of the Berlin year, however, was an encounter with a fellow countryman, Robert Kajanus, who came to Berlin to conduct the first performance of his 'Aino' Symphony. This opened Sibelius's eyes to the potentialities of Finnish mythology and was an immediate source of inspiration for the 'Kullervo' Symphony, which he completed two years later. Their meeting was to have more than immediate consequences. At this time, Kajanus was known primarily as a composer, but in later years he concentrated more and more on conducting and became the outstanding interpreter of Sibelius's music. His understanding of the orchestra was of enormous value to Sibelius, who drew greatly on his advice.

As far as composition was concerned, apart from the G minor Piano Quintet, Sibelius had comparatively little to show for his Berlin year. To tell the truth, the Prussian atmosphere of the German capital was not entirely congenial to him, and he came to feel much happier in the more easy-going atmosphere of Vienna. Before proceeding there, however, he returned to Finland for the summer.

20

J. Sibelius.

Kustaa II Aadolf, protestanttisuuden perustaja

Kustaa II. Aadolf, Ruotsin kuningas, oli saanut sotaisan, ja siihen ai-kaan kaksoen erinomaisen kasvatuksen jo nuorena seura-si hän Horn'ia, luotettavaa sotapäällikköä, hänen ret-killään Itämeren maakunnissa. Näillä veti nuori Kustaa huomi-ota puoleensa sekä uljuudellaan että mielenjaloutensa kautta, joka erittäin tuli näkyviin hänen kohdellessa vangittuita vihollisi-a.

Overleaf: 18 The family trio, Jean, Linda and Christian, 1889. 19 The violin class, with Sibelius in the background, at Helsinki School of Music. 20 Helsinki School of Music, as it was in the 1880s. 21 Tsar Alexander University

18 20
19 21

He spent most of the time with the Järnefelts, Armas having introduced him to his family when he came to Helsinki four years before. The family was an influential one: the father was a general and had for some time been Governor of some of the provinces in Inner Finland; his wife was an admirer of Tolstoy and a feminist; one son, Arvid, became an important literary figure; and Armas, who was four years younger than Sibelius, became well-known as a composer, particularly of lighter genre pieces, as well as being a fine conductor. There was one daughter, Aino, and she and Sibelius became secretly engaged before his return to the continent in the autumn.

Sibelius wanted to study with Brahms in Vienna, and had persuaded Busoni to provide him with a letter of recommendation. Brahms, however, was not at this stage in his life much interested in teaching anyone, no matter how gifted they might be, and the plan failed. (The two composers did eventually meet some months later at the Café Leidinger, one of Brahms's favourite haunts.) This must have been a great disappointment to Sibelius, but he was well connected in Vienna and armed with a formidable collection of introductory letters. He was fortunate enough to be accepted by Karl Goldmark, a composer much in favour with the Viennese public, who rarely accepted composition pupils. Wegelius's letter of introduction must have been persuasive, and Sibelius himself was enormously flattered when Goldmark agreed to his request for help in studying orchestration by saying, 'I am very happy to give advice to the young artist.' It was the first time Sibelius had been addressed as an 'artist'. Goldmark's teaching, however, was confined to some consultation lessons – he subjected Sibelius's first orchestral essay, an overture, to thorough scrutiny – and it was left to Hans Richter (who many years later presented the Second Symphony to Hallé audiences) to recommend the young Finn to Robert Fuchs, a trained orchestrator and a prolific composer of the Brahmsian falange. In general Sibelius worked much harder in Vienna than he had done the previous year in Berlin. Apart from another orchestral overture, he wrote a piano quartet in C and began an octet, whose themes furnished the material for *En Saga* two years later. Also dating from the Viennese year are a number of songs, three of them included in the Seven Runeberg settings, op. 13.

The 'Kullervo' Symphony On his return home in the summer of 1891, Sibelius joined his family at Loviisa and, apart from regular trips to Helsinki, stayed there for the bulk of the year, working on the various projects he had begun in Vienna and also on the 'Kullervo' Symphony. This is a vast fresco on Mahlerian scale that takes some seventy-five to eighty minutes in performance and calls for two soloists and male chorus. When it was first given in April 1892, it was an enormous success, both with the public and with the critics. Sibelius himself conducted, and from that moment onwards his position in Finnish musical life was never seriously challenged. This was the first individual and commanding voice in Finnish music. The orchestra was, of course, the ideal medium for giving expression to the world of Finnish mythology which had fascinated him throughout his teens. If the *Kalevala*, along with Snellman's language reform, had awoken the Finns to their own culture and fostered a spirit of nationalism which continued to grow all through the second half of the century, Sibelius's 'Kullervo', along with other nationalist music that he composed in the 1890s, did much to keep that spirit alive.

Despite its inevitable immaturity and somewhat faltering proportions, what is so striking about the 'Kullervo' Symphony is the astonishing assurance of its orchestration and the immediate sense of identity it imparts. The very opening bars proclaim that this is a new voice and an independent personality in European music. There may be legitimate reservations about the work as a whole, but there can be no doubts about the forward sweep of the first movement. Here is the feel of a genuine symphonist. Taken in its entirety, the seams in its structure are clearly visible; but equally evident is its grasp of form and sense of movement, even if its formal mastery is imperfect. There are interesting orchestral devices (the effect of the repeated oboe notes during the development of the first movement is highly original), some of which he chose never to take further. Much the most substantial movement is the third, *Kullervo and his Sister*, in which there is some dramatic writing of the highest quality and a magnificent coda when Kullervo realizes the incestuous character of the relationship in which he has been involved, and laments the death of his sister.

The vocal writing in this lengthy movement, the centre-piece of the whole work, suggests that Sibelius could well have developed an extremely respectable operatic style had he chosen to do so. Indeed, he did subsequently attempt two operas: a year after 'Kullervo', in 1893, he began work on *Veneen luominen (The Building of the Boat)*, to his own libretto based on the *Kalevala*, for which his tone-poem *The Swan of Tuonela* was originally intended; and some four years later, in 1896, he wrote *Jungfrun i tornet (The Maiden in the Tower)*. Neither opera has been published, so there is no way of establishing the full extent of Wagner's influence. We know that Wegelius's enthusiasm for Wagner met with little response from his pupil, although he was cautious and tactful in his

Overleaf:
22 Sibelius, *c.* 1888.
23 Wegelius
on the verandah of
his villa at Kuusisaari

25

23

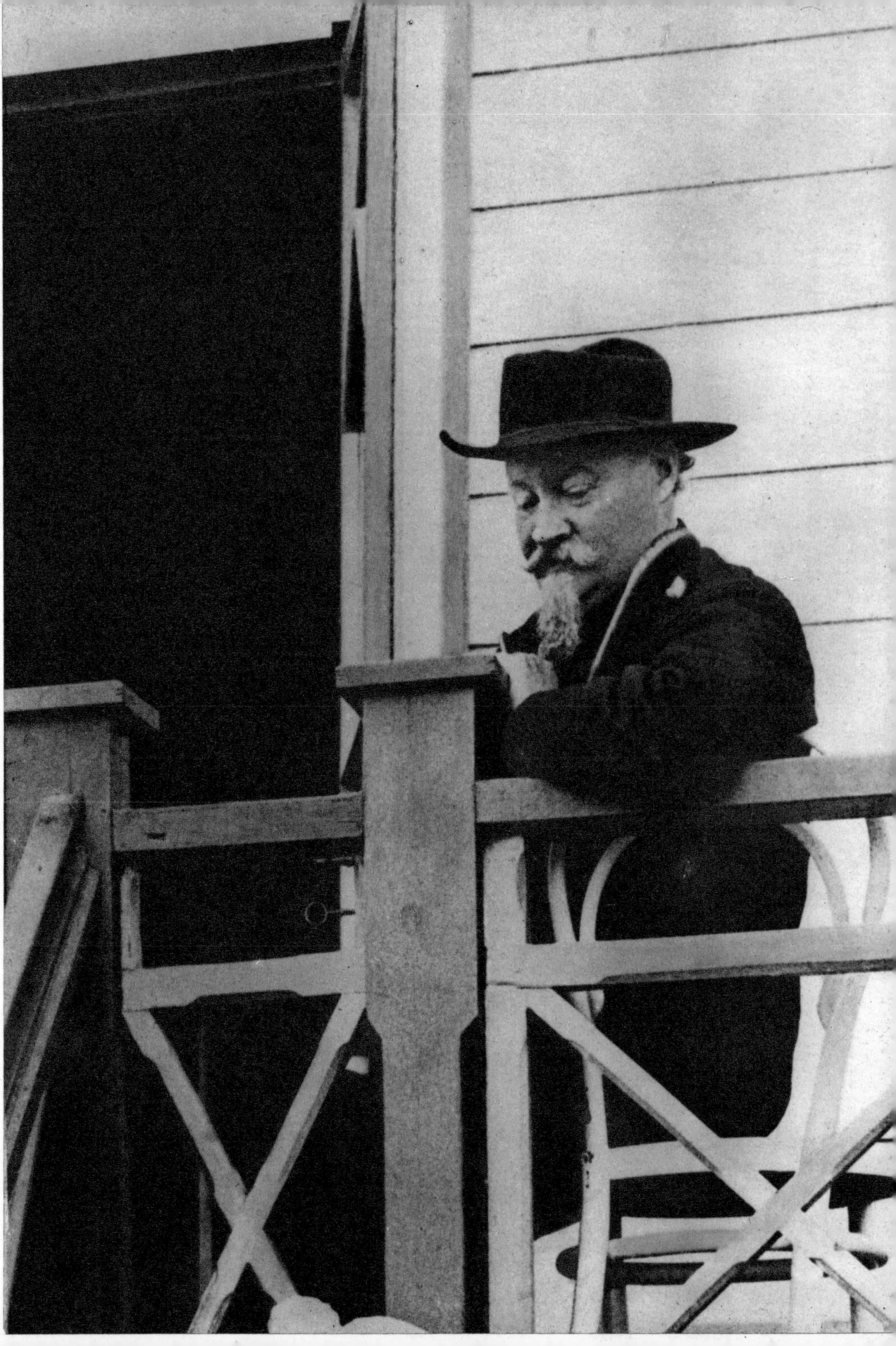

25 Adolf Paul, author of
King Christian II, 1895

26 Busoni, aged 12, five
years after his début

letters from Berlin, where he heard performances of *Tannhäuser* and *Die Meistersinger*. Armas Järnefelt dragged him off to Bayreuth in 1894, and for all Sibelius's denunciation of Wagner both in print and verbally, his influence was such as to be inescapable at this period. It is difficult to believe that *The Maiden in the Tower* escaped this influence. Certainly some of the songs that he wrote later, in particular the scena *Höstkväll* (1903), reveal touches that would have been impossible without Wagner's example, though in general he had little direct impact on Sibelius's melodic style or harmonic vocabulary.

The success of 'Kullervo' was followed by two important events. *The period* First, in June 1892, his marriage to Aino Järnefelt. No doubt the im- *1893–5* mense public acclaim he had received facilitated a match which brought him into one of the most influential Finnish-speaking families in the country. The second was a commission from Kajanus for an orchestral work, and the result was *En Saga*.

En Saga met with a cool reception at its first performance in 1893 and

29

◀ 24 Karl Flodin, who was one of the first to recognize Sibelius's talent

28   Elisabeth Järnefelt, Sibelius's mother-in-law

27   Armas Järnefelt

Sibelius quickly withdrew it for revision. The final version did not appear until 1902, by which time he had acquired much greater mastery. The two versions afford a valuable insight into the way in which this growing mastery, both of the orchestra and of form, showed itself. He feels sufficiently sure of himself, for example, to elongate his pedal points in the second version, rather than contract them as one might have expected. In the first version the longest pedal note is sustained for sixty bars, and in the second it is lengthened to eighty-two. Similarly, he reduced the number of key changes in the revision, rather than the opposite. And, finally, the familiar *divisi* strings that open the work are much more imaginatively scored in the second version: in the first, these passages are not at all successful.

Also in 1893, Sibelius received a commission from the Viipuri Students' Union for incidental music for a series of historical tableaux. The result was the *Karelia* music, an overture (op. 10) and the suite of three movements (op. 11), one of his best-known works, which he later

published for concert performance. Oddly enough, several contemporary critics had affected to detect the influence of Karelian folk music in the 'Kullervo' Symphony; but Sibelius did not visit Karelia until later, shortly after his marriage, to make the acquaintance of these supposed influences. 'First I composed "Kullervo",' he told Ekman; 'then I went to Karelia to hear, for the first time in my life, the *Kalevala* runes from the lips of the people. This may seem strange, but it was actually the case.' In any event, the stride forward from 'Kullervo' and the first version of *En Saga,* on the one hand, to *Karelia,* on the other, was a considerable one in terms of orchestral assurance.

It was transformed into a positive leap forward only a few months later, in *The Swan of Tuonela.* The period 1893–5 was a prolific one: songs, piano music, the cantata *Vårsång (Springsong),* all date from these years; but in sheer imaginative breadth none can match this set of four tone-poems based on Lemminkäinen's adventures as described in the *Kalevala.* His earlier works from 'Kullervo' to the *Karelia* music had

29 Runeberg Esplanade, Helsinki about 1900, showing the Kämp Hotel (second from the right), one of the places where Sibelius and Busoni used to meet

Overleaf:
30 Richard Strauss.
31 Hans von Bülow.
32 Albert Becker, Sibelius's teacher in Berlin.
33 Joseph Joachim.
34 Sibelius in Berlin

31

shown promise of great mastery, but *The Swan of Tuonela* is the first sign of absolute genius. There had been no sound like this in music before. From the very first chords there is a chilling intensity and imaginative vision of the highest order.

The 'Four Legends'

The 'Four Legends', or the 'Lemminkäinen Suite' as it is sometimes called, was completed at the turn of 1895–6, and Sibelius included the work at a concert of his own music in the following April. The four Legends were then given in the following order: *Lemminkäinen and the Maidens of the Island, Lemminkäinen in Tuonela, The Swan of Tuonela* and *The Return of Lemminkäinen.* Sibelius was not only an immensely self-critical artist, but intensely responsive to criticism from others. When they were first performed, the Legends were received unfavourably by Karl Flodin, who had been a champion of Sibelius's art and whose opinion the composer would naturally respect. Sibelius revised the pieces yet again, and presented them in their new form at a concert in the following year. On this occasion Flodin wrote, 'I am no Hanslick, but I must admit that such music as the Lemminkäinen Suite disheartens me, makes me troubled and distressed. Is it music's task to evoke such moods?' In a sense this was prompted less by the quality of the music than by the feeling that Sibelius was moving into the fashionable realm of programme music and away from the purely symphonic tradition for which he seemed so well endowed. In any event, he further revised *The Swan* and *The Return of Lemminkäinen,* and withheld the remaining two from publication. He apparently released the manuscripts to the Kalevala Society and only sanctioned their performance (after further revision) in the 1930s.

Listening now to the two Legends over which he hesitated so long, one is astonished by their richness of invention and originality: the very opening chord of *Lemminkäinen and the Maidens* establishes this striking individuality. Vaughan Williams once observed that true originality lies in the ability to make the simplest and most ordinary chord sound totally individual. This capacity Sibelius possessed in a unique degree: the most commonplace chord

35 August Stindberg, whom Sibelius greatly admired

34

36 Aino Järnefelt, later Sibelius's wife ▶

37   Old Vienna. On the right,

sounds immediately Sibelian in his hands. And there can be few more original or exciting pieces than *The Return of Lemminkäinen,* an exhilarating *moto perpetuo* that vividly describes Lemminkäinen's progress as he gallops furiously through the wild forest landscape of the Northland. A stunning piece of virtuosity, this, that forms an admirable foil to the brooding, dark intensity of *Lemminkäinen in Tuonela,* by whose side it was originally placed.

Although *The Swan* and *The Return of Lemminkäinen* exhibit not a trace of Russian influence, the first of the Legends, *Lemminkäinen and the Maidens,* does. At times it suggests the Russians in general (represented by Balakirev), at others Tchaikovsky in particular. Tchaikovsky's influence had already been discernible in the slow movement of 'Kullervo' (another work, incidentally, that Sibelius had withdrawn despite its enormous public success), and it is interesting to note that St Petersburg was considered, along with Berlin and Vienna, when the question of studying abroad first arose. Tchaikovsky's influence on Sibelius is most noticeable in the finale of the First Symphony or the slow movement of the same work, and persisted in some of his lighter music until quite late in his career. The second movement of the post-war *Suite mignonne,* for instance, could easily have stepped out of a divertissement from a Tchaikovsky ballet score, though its accents are distinctly Nordic.

To return to Flodin's criticism of the 'Four Legends', it is worth

the Wiedner Hauptstrasse, the street on which Sibelius lived

bearing in mind that Finland at this time was longing for a symphonist. Up till then, there was no Finnish symphony of note, and Scandinavia as a whole had not yet produced a symphonic tradition of any significance. Gade's symphonies were too indebted to Leipzig and Mendelssohn, Berwald's had yet to be 'discovered', and the time was ripe for a composer to do for Scandinavian music what Ibsen, Strindberg and Björnson were achieving, or were to achieve, for Scandinavian drama. A gifted young Finnish composer, Ernst Mielck, who had studied with Bruch in Berlin and whose career was tragically cut short at the age of twenty, essayed a symphony in 1897, a work which was lavishly praised – praise, one suspects, more for the attempt than the achievement, and also, perhaps, with a view to encouraging Sibelius to take up the gauntlet. In any event, Sibelius, whose formal instincts were astonishingly strong, was given an added impulse to turn to the symphony.

State grant

Even though one of his works, the choral version of *Rakastava,* had failed to win a prize in a competition (it came second, the first prize being awarded to a piece by Genetz), and despite the reverses suffered by the 'Four Legends', Sibelius was recognized as the leading figure in Finnish music. His position was challenged only by Kajanus, ten years his senior and an established conductor and composer. But it was Sibelius and not Kajanus who, in 1896, was elected to fill the vacancy left by the retirement of Faltin as Professor of Music at the University. Subsequently

37

41 Anton Bruckner

42 Richard Wagner

the election was reversed, a good deal of heat generated and Kajanus appointed in his stead. The politics behind the appointment are too complex to be recounted here, but the outcome was eventually to Sibelius's advantage. In view of the loss of this position, his admirers, both in Turku (where the two better-known Legends were well received in the spring of 1898) and in Helsinki, persuaded the Senate to grant him a salary roughly equivalent to what he would have earned in the teaching post. Thus, at the age of thirty-two, he became the recipient of a grant for life of 3,000 Finnmarks a year (roughly £850) – an arrangement which showed extraordinary enlightenment on the part of the Finnish government. In fact, he still did a certain amount of teaching to supple-

39

◀ 38, 39, 40 Left, Brahms, with whom Sibelius had hoped to study at Vienna. Right, Karl Goldmark, who gave Sibelius some consultation lessons. The Vienna Opera, as it was in the 1890s

ment his income, for he now had a family of two children as well as expensive tastes, but at least he was able to devote the bulk of his time to composition. As a result, the years at the end of the century were rich ones, producing not only songs and incidental music for the theatre, but the first of his seven symphonies.

The music to *King Christian II,* the play by his friend Adolf Paul, comes from this time. It was his first work for the theatre and, together with *Finlandia* and *Valse triste,* laid the foundations for his popularity abroad. Sir Henry Wood and other conductors gave it frequently in the first years of the present century, and the Grieg-like quality of the *Elegy* as well as the gentle playfulness of the *Musette* won Sibelius many admirers. A letter from Sibelius to Paul serves as a useful reminder of the limited resources that were open to him – or any Finnish composer – at that time. Speaking of the *Musette,* he said: 'It should be for bagpipes and reeds, but I've scored it for two clarinets and two bassoons. Extravagant, isn't it? We have only two bassoon players in the entire country and one of them is consumptive. But my music won't be too hard on him: I'll see to that.' Later on, for concert purposes, Sibelius added three movements for a larger ensemble.

With the success of the *King Christian* music, Sibelius was commissioned to write another series of orchestral pieces for a historical and patriotic pageant. The *Scènes historiques,* as they are known, are more ambitious in scope than the *Karelia* music that he had composed some years earlier, and arose in a more complex context. During the nineteenth century, Finland had been kept on a fairly loose rein by the Tsarist authorities, but as the movement for national self-determination grew, so the government felt obliged to tighten its hold. With the accession to the throne of Tsar Nicholas II in 1894, the Russians began to introduce repressive legislation: the relatively liberal government in Finland was replaced by that of General Bobrikov, who in 1899, introduced the so-called February manifesto, severely curtailing the right of assembly and virtually crippling Finnish autonomy. The November 1899 pageant for which Sibelius composed his music was given in aid of the Press Pension Fund, but beneath the innocuous surface lay strong nationalistic undertones. Various episodes in Finnish history were depicted, and the Prelude to the last scene of all was the famous *Finlandia.* The enormous success enjoyed by this piece is attributable to the climate of national feeling which it so admirably gauged, rather than to its musical excellence: musically, it bears much the same relationship to Sibelius's serious works as do the *Pomp and Circumstance* marches to

40

43 Robert Kajanus, one of Sibelius's most influential supporters

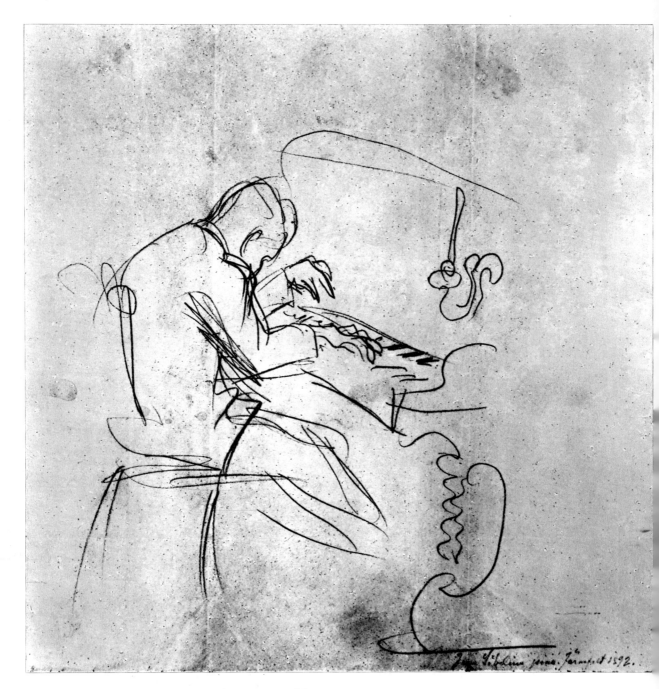

44   Sibelius at the piano, a drawing by Eero Järnefelt

Elgar's, or the '1812 Overture' to Tchaikovsky's. For all its Lisztian rhetoric, it would be idle to pretend that it equals the other pieces in the set such as *At the Drawbridge* or that astonishingly powerful (but neglected) composition, *The Chase*.

Like Brahms, Sibelius hesitated before turning to the symphony. Although 'Kullervo' is popularly known as a symphony, the composer certainly did not regard it as such, and took care to call it 'a symphonic poem for soprano, baritone, male chorus and orchestra'. The First Symphony proper was not finished until Sibelius was in his thirty-fourth year and occupied him for most of the autumn of 1898. He himself conducted its first performance in Helsinki in April 1899. The 1890s had seen him grow steadily as a master of the orchestra, and the contrast between 'Kullervo' and the First Symphony shows just how far he had advanced. The contrast between 'Kullervo' and, say, the 'Four Legends', in particular *The Swan of Tuonela,* was striking enough (though misleading, since Sibelius revised the Legends); when one comes to the First Symphony, the change is of a different order. Whereas in 'Kullervo' one glimpses an orchestral imagination of striking talent, there are few instances when one feels that Sibelius's ideas are inseparable from the instrumental colouring in which he has clothed them. The hallmark of the great masters of the orchestra, like Berlioz, Wagner and Debussy, is the capacity to conceive ideas wholly in terms of the genius of a particular instrument or group of instruments, so that the musical line and the instrumental colouring which clothes it become indivisible. In this sense the First Symphony marks Sibelius's emergence as a master of the orchestra; for it would be impossible to divorce such an idea as the second group of the first movement from its orchestral colouring.

The First Symphony is a work that sums up the classical-romantic symphony rather than looks forward to the twentieth century. Its slow movement echoes the world of Tchaikovsky's *Pathétique,* written only a few years earlier (though there are some highly individual strokes, such as the E flat ostinato pedal point on the harp at the very beginning of the movement). The finale, too, in its sheer melodic vitality, has a Tchaikovskian generosity of feeling. But the first movement reveals a compactness of form and an organizing ability that goes further than anything in the Tchaikovsky symphonies; indeed, in terms of formal perfection, it is comparable only with the finest examples of its time.

It was this symphony, together with *Finlandia,* that the Helsinki City Orchestra under Kajanus took with them on their European tour the following year. They visited Stockholm, Copenhagen, Lübeck,

43

Till Förlags aktiebolaget Otava öfverlåter jag härmed förlagsrätten, utan vilkor, till tusen (1000) exemplar af "7 sånger af Runeberg i musik satta af Jean Sibelius".

Helsingfors den 21 Decemb. 1892.

Jean Sibelius.

45 A letter from Sibelius to his publisher, giving him the rights in the 'Runeberg Songs'

46 Title-page of the 'Runeberg Songs', the first of Sibelius's works to be published

47 The artist Akseli Gallén-Kallela, one of Sibelius's friends

Hamburg and, finally, Paris, where their concerts formed part of the Finnish contribution to the Paris Exhibition of 1900. The tour, the first of its kind by the orchestra, was primarily a demonstration of national feeling, and its backers included one of Sibelius's loyalest friends and a most generous patron of the arts, Baron Axel Carpelan. Shortly after the Helsinki Orchestra's tour, Carpelan settled on Sibelius enough money to enable him to take a year off from his teaching commitments and go with his family to Italy. He stayed in Italy from autumn 1901 to spring 1902, renting a villa in Rapallo, and devoted himself entirely to composition. It was during these months that he worked on the Second *The Second* Symphony, which he finished early that winter, returning to Finland to *Symphony* conduct its first performance in March. Like Ibsen, Sibelius had a

46

lifelong love for Italy; not only the Second Symphony and other smaller works were written there, but also that most uncompromisingly Arctic of all his symphonic masterpieces, *Tapiola*. As a gesture of thanks, Sibelius dedicated the new symphony to Carpelan.

The Second Symphony (1902) strikes a more overtly nationalist stance than any of Sibelius's other symphonies, and the patriotic fervour of its finale is as immediate as it is stirring. In a sense, this work breathes much the same air as its predecessor: it is a national-romantic symphony that on superficial acquaintance looks back to the nineteenth century rather than forward to later developments. With its full-blooded rhetoric and lushness of idiom, it conveys a sunny, relaxed atmosphere, but this geniality hides a granite-like strength of structure. The first movement

48 Gallén-Kallela's painting *Symposium*, which caused something of a scandal. Sibelius and Kajanus are shown at the table, while the artist himself appears standing

Overleaf: 49 Programme of a concert given by the Helsinki Orchestra in Amsterdam, including music by Sibelius. 50 Closing bars of Sibelius's *Black Roses*. 51 Ida Ekman, one of the most brilliant interpreters of his songs

is a good deal more remarkable than at first sight it seems. Indeed, in the 1930s, Cecil Gray declared that Sibelius broke entirely new ground in this movement: that in the exposition he gives us no more than melodic strands, which only later grow into melodies and are drawn together in their complete form in the restatement. This is not, in fact, quite the case: the movement does not depart in its main outlines from the ground plan of sonata form; rather, its ideas unfold in such a way as to be barely susceptible to formal analysis.

Whatever the formal subtleties may be, there can be no question about the quality or the directness of thematic appeal in both the first movement and the second. Oddly enough, the famous oboe melody in the trio of the scherzo, which could hardly sound more nationalistic, is said to be of Czech origin. On his travels in 1901 Sibelius passed through Prague, where he took the opportunity of renewing his acquaintance with Suk, Dvořák's son-in-law, as well as meeting Dvořák himself, and he may have run across this melody then. None of the other three movements displays the degree of organic complexity of the first; least of all the finale, which is probably the simplest symphonic finale that Sibelius ever wrote. There is, in any event, no doubt about its patriotic overtones or the full-bloodedness of its inspiration; indeed, given an exciting performance, it assumes heroic, rather than merely patriotic, proportions.

Songs   These years, at the turn of the century, were rich also in other music, some of it, like *Atenarnas sång (Song of the Athenians),* overtly patriotic, and some of it, like *The Origin of Fire,* which showed his continuing interest in the *Kalevala,* more indirect in its nationalism. Moreover, the most famous of his songs, as well as some of his finest, date from this period. Sibelius's achievement as a symphonist tends to overshadow his output in other fields. All in all, he composed about a hundred songs, though only a handful of them have achieved any measure of popularity. Most of them are settings of poets writing in Swedish; surprisingly few are to Finnish texts. Sibelius seems to have turned to Finnish when writing for choir, in particular male choir. He was deeply inspired by the lyric nature poetry of Runeberg, whom Brahms also admired, and some of his finest songs are to his poetry. Almost a quarter of his vocal output is to Runeberg, while for the rest he turned to the Swedish poets, Viktor Rydberg and Gustaf Fröding, or to his own countrymen and contemporaries, Tavaststjerna and Wecksell. *Svarta rosor (Black Roses)* is perhaps the best known of all his songs, though it is far from being the most characteristic or powerful. Both *Black Roses* and *Säv, säv, susa (Sigh sedges, sigh!)* belong to the 1899 set of six songs, op. 36, while one of his

most ambitious songs, *Höstkväll (Autumn Evening),* was written in 1903, only a few months after the Second Symphony.

52 Manuscript of 'Kullervo'

One reason why the songs have not reached a wider audience is the inaccessibility of the Scandinavian languages to non-native singers. Much the same is true of Mussorgsky's songs, which would be far more often played were they not so intimately connected with the Russian language. Language has not generally stood in the way of Grieg's songs, for these are usually sung in translation, but even so masterly a song-cycle as *Haugtussa* rarely figures in the recital room. Another factor is the comparative unadventurousness of the piano parts, for Sibelius did not write idiomatically for the keyboard, as did Nielsen. His piano writing is a good deal more effective than, say, Berwald's, but it pales by the side of his instinctive, masterly handling of the orchestra. This is clearly illustrated if one compares the two versions of *Autumn Evening,* the original for voice and piano, and the later orchestral version. Whereas the former is merely competent, the latter, half song, half operatic *scena,* is supremely successful; Rydberg's poem dealing with the solitary wanderer exulting in the power and majesty of nature struck a responsive chord in the composer. For Sibelius, too, one feels, the relationship with nature is a predominant one, as was the preoccupation with mythology; both nature and myth interest him more deeply than the tensions arising from human relationships. (The world both of *The Swan of Tuonela* and of the much later *Tapiola* is totally unpeopled.) The atmosphere of the orchestral version of *Autumn Evening* could hardly be more powerfully evoked and looks forward to such works as *The Bard,* one of his most impressive nature poems, while in the freedom of its vocal line it even suggests *Luonnotar.*

Another work on which Sibelius was engaged at this time was the Violin Concerto, perhaps the most popular of all his major works. Its opening is certainly one of his most inspired, of a quality that silences criticism. Its failure to live up to the promise of the opening has no parallel elsewhere in Sibelius's major works, for he does not belong to that category of composer whose opening ideas are more striking than their fulfilment. He finished the first draft in 1903, but he was not satisfied with it and, as in the case of so many of his earlier works, withdrew it for revision after its first performance; this was in 1904, with Viktor Nováček as soloist. In its definitive form it was heard the following year, with Richard Strauss conducting.

International reputation Strauss was not alone among famous contemporaries to admire and present Sibelius's works. Busoni included the Second Symphony in his 1905 series of concerts in Berlin, and Hans Richter conducted its first performance at a Hallé Concert in England. If in the 1890s Sibelius's reputation as Finland's leading composer became established in his own country, in the next decade it began to be recognized abroad. Henry Wood introduced the *King Christian II* music to England in 1901, and Granville Bantock, one of Sibelius's greatest champions at this time, conducted the first performance of the First Symphony four years later. *Finlandia* had begun its triumphant concert-hall career, and already in the 1890s Sibelius had been introduced by his friend Adolf Paul to the Leipzig publishers Breitkopf and Härtel, who added his name to their catalogue.

It was to Breitkopf and Härtel that Sibelius sold the rights of *Valse triste* – for the trifling sum of three hundred marks, a decision which he was to regret for the rest of his life. *Valse triste* comes from the incidental music to *Kuolema,* a play by his brother-in-law Arvid Järnefelt, a few years his senior and a writer much influenced by Tolstoy. Of the six pieces he wrote for the play, *Valse triste* leapt into immediate and lasting popularity; indeed, it has become so familiar that one tends to overlook its genuine originality. The piece was played during the scene in which the main character, Paavali, sleeps by the bedside of his dying mother. He dreams that Death comes, and that his mother, mistaking the visitor for her dead husband, dances with him; Paavali wakes up and finds his mother dead. One can imagine how haunting *Valse triste* must have seemed when its impact was still fresh. A by-product of its success was Sibelius's determination to compose another work of this kind and secure a steady income from it. He continued to write a good deal of light music during the rest of his life, but failed to repeat the success of *Valse triste,* which made a small fortune for Breitkopf.

In addition to Bantock and Wood, Sibelius's English admirers included the critics Ernest Newman and Rosa Newmarch, especially the latter. Newmarch, who was in her mid-forties at this time, was already well-known as a champion of Slav and Czech music. She had written studies of Borodin and Tchaikovsky, and had been to St Petersburg in 1897 to work at the Imperial Library under Stassov. She became not only one of Sibelius's most active champions, but a good friend, and the two corresponded for many years. It was to her that Sibelius wrote of his taste for the countryside, where, unhampered by social obligations, he undoubtedly worked more quickly and effectively than in the Finnish capital. In 1904 he bought some land and had a villa built at the little village of Järvenpää, some thirty-five kilometres north-east of Helsinki. He named the villa Ainola, after his wife. In the autumn of the same year he received an invitation to visit England, but postponed the trip when he received a commission from his friend the poet Bertil Gripenberg to write some incidental music for the Swedish translation of Maeterlinck's *Pelléas and Mélisande.* When he eventually visited England, he seems to have liked it: he was so liberally entertained by Bantock and his friends that he was, as he put it, 'unable to make the acquaintance of the English coinage'. He continued to travel widely, and work on the Third Symphony, begun in 1904, progressed slowly. While in London he met Wood, and agreed to come to London in the spring of 1907 to direct the symphony's first performance.

The year 1905 saw social unrest spread throughout Tsarist Russia, including Finland, culminating in the abortive October uprising in St Petersburg. Russia's war against Japan had resulted in a humiliating defeat, and had added further burdens on the Russian peasantry, who were already sufficiently oppressed by a reactionary and backward ruling class. Finnish nationalists and intellectuals watched with sympathy every movement towards liberalization in Russia, and even gave practical help to revolutionaries and writers persecuted by the Tsarist regime, including Gorki. For Sibelius, however, both at home and abroad, it was a highly successful year. In France, he received the highest tribute, being made a member of the Legion of Honour. Moreover, it was a period of great productivity. The Third Symphony, admittedly, was developing slowly, but the exquisite music to *Pelléas and Mélisande* belongs to 1905, and was followed by one of Sibelius's most neglected but poetic scores for the theatre, the music to *Belshazzar's Feast,* a play by his friend Hjalmar Procopé. This and *Pohjola's Daughter,* one of the greatest of his symphonic poems, date from 1906.

The symphonic poem was still at the height of fashion at the turn of the century, and in Richard Strauss it had found its greatest master. This essentially romantic musical form introduced literary and pictorial elements into the symphonic tradition of thematic development. Sibelius's contribution to the symphonic poem, no less remarkable than his achievement as a symphonist, was to combine firm structural discipline with poetic imagination of the highest order. *Pohjola's Daughter,* like nearly all Sibelius's symphonic poems, draws on the *Kalevala* for its inspiration, and unites symphonic economy with the most striking and imaginative inspiration. Its story tells of Väinämöinen's attempts to woo the Maid of Pohjola, for whose icy charms he has fallen. She sets him various impossible tasks, among them tying an egg into invisible knots and making a boat from the fragments of her spindle, which he tries to do but fails. No other tone-poem is so explicit in the narrative sense (one cannot help feeling that the example of Strauss was close at hand), and yet no other is so formally perfect. Thus, it can make perfect musical sense even if the listener is totally ignorant of its programmatic content. Sibelius conducted it for the first time in December 1906, on a visit to St Petersburg. Also at this time he began work on *Nightride and Sunrise,* one of his least played symphonic poems, which he completed in 1907.

The Third Symphony The Third Symphony continued to make slow progress – so slow, in fact, that its first performance, planned for March 1907, had to be postponed. It eventually saw the light of day at a concert in Helsinki in

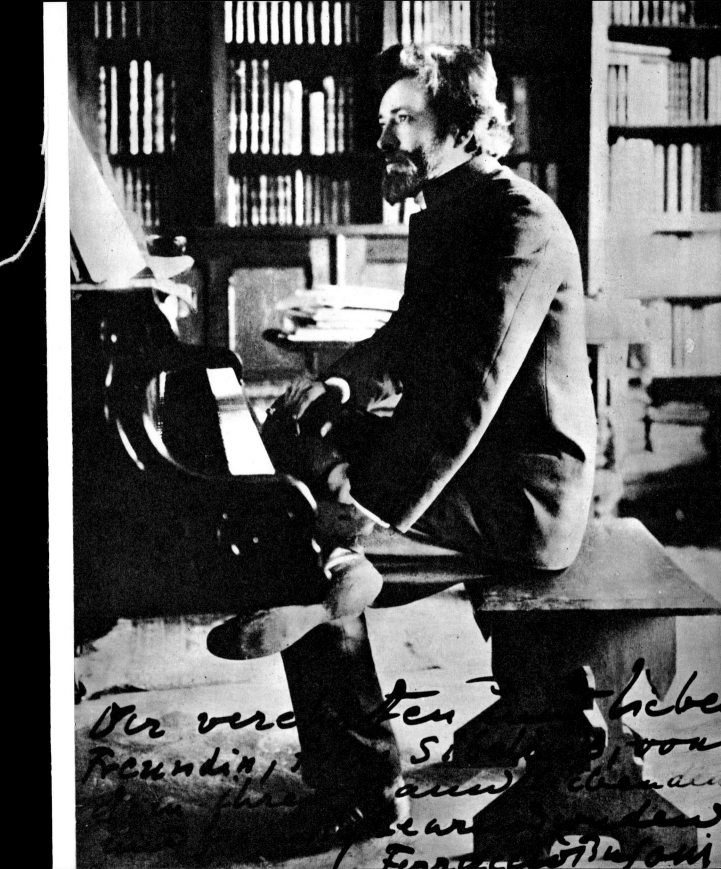

the autumn of 1907; its British première took place in 1908, at a concert given by the Royal Philharmonic Society, and Sibelius made a special trip to London to conduct it. As a token of his gratitude for Bantock's championship (and hospitality), he dedicated the work to him. It is, of course, idle to pretend that a composer's style suddenly changes, and Sibelius's style developed more consistently than is generally acknowledged. *Autumn Evening* is an example of the austere nature poet whom one associates with *Luonnotar* or *The Bard,* who co-existed, as it were, with the full-blooded romantic of the Second Symphony. In the output of most composers, various trends co-exist before one or the other becomes predominant. However, as far as the symphonies are concerned,

56

one can be forgiven for regarding the Third as singularly classical by the side of so passionate a work as its predecessor.

The contrast between the Third and the symphonies of Mahler could hardly be more striking. It was during Mahler's visit to Helsinki in 1907, when the Third Symphony was approaching completion, that the two composers met, and that their famous – and revealing – conversation took place. Mahler attended a popular concert which included work by Sibelius, and, to judge by a letter he wrote to his wife, did not form a high opinion of what he heard. However, the following morning, when Sibelius called on him at his hotel, he formed a more favourable impression of the Finnish composer. Their meeting is described by Sibelius's biographer, Karl Ekman, who records Sibelius as saying: 'When our conversation touched on the symphony, I said that I admired the style and severity of the form, and the profound logic that created an inner connection between the motifs. This was my experience in the course of my creative work. Mahler's opinion was just the opposite. "No!" he said. "The symphony must be like the world; it must be all-embracing." '

Illness and the Fourth
The Fourth Symphony and the austere works that followed it, like *The Bard* and *Luonnotar,* are obviously the product of a bitter spiritual experience and can be related in some measure to Sibelius's illness. In 1908 he began to be increasingly troubled by pains in the throat, and eventually a tumour was diagnosed. He was at this time at the height of his powers, and the thought that he had a cancer of the throat was a terrible shock. Although in actual fact he was to live almost fifty years longer, death seemed uncomfortably close; he had, moreover, three children and a fourth on the way. He underwent a series of operations to remove the growth, and for many years the knowledge that a further, fatal tumour might develop must have weighed heavily on his mind. Although his music already shows a disposition to economy in, say, the first movement of the First Symphony, this tendency becomes still more marked in the period 1908–13, and persists in nearly all the major works he wrote afterwards.

In the Fourth Symphony one feels that Sibelius, having looked into the abyss, was driven by an intensified sense of creative urgency to concentrate on barest essentials. Its severity and bleakness earned the Fourth the title of the 'Barkbröd' Symphony, a reference to times of hardship in the nineteenth century when the peasants were forced to use the bark of trees for making bread. At its first performances in Scandinavia and elsewhere in Europe, it bewildered and puzzled the public; at its

58

56 Richard Strauss with Georg Schnéevoigt,
a well-known interpreter of Sibelius's work

première in Gothenburg it was hissed and booed by the audience, while in America it evoked all sorts of hostile criticism. It is a work that offers no false consolation, the hard facts of nature's unremitting hostility and indifference are immutable. Only once, in the slow movement, does resistance to nature's hardness release itself in a passionate, song-like protest, a moment of glowing, powerful warmth. Yet, taken as a whole, the opening movement is the most densely concentrated, bleak and uncompromising of the whole work. The dark, searching preamble, with the pendulum-like motion of the double-basses swinging back and forth between F sharp and E, over which the solitary cello utters its desolate A minor tune, soon establishes the mood. I can think of few precedents in symphonic literature for an opening of this kind, and few instances when the initial motive of four notes permeates the thematic substance of a movement at all levels so completely and yet so unobtrusively. Nor does the searching, angular writing in the development have many parallels outside such avant-garde composers of the day as Bartók, Schönberg and Busoni. Sibelius himself spoke of the symphony as 'a protest against the trends of our time', and there is certainly none of the glittering orchestral sonorities of a Strauss or a Ravel.

A great deal has been written about Sibelius's feeling for nature, and few composers, save perhaps Debussy in *Nuages* and *La Mer,* achieve a greater degree of intimacy or identification with it. Nature – and man's relationship with it – is one of the central themes of his art, and the opening of the slow movement of the Fourth Symphony conveys both the intimacy and the spaciousness of nature with extraordinary intensity. Both here and in the Sixth Symphony we glimpse something of the luminous pallor of the Scandinavian summer, with its white nights and delicate colourings. The terseness and economy of the scherzo of the Fourth – he telescopes the reprise into a mere six bars! – are typical of Sibelius at this time. *The Bard,* a tone-poem of the utmost concentration of mood, has a similar terse simplicity of musical substance. It is, moreover, one of Sibelius's most elusive scores, rich in atmosphere and interesting in its formal layout; in its change of mood half-way through, it almost suggests the sonnet.

Another case of extreme compression (though in its effect totally different from *The Bard*) is the set of three piano sonatinas, op. 67, in the first of which the outline of a sonata-style movement is cast in a few simple brush-strokes, the whole movement lasting about one-and-a-half minutes. Sibelius's output of piano music, incidentally, is considerable; it is, however, almost consistently inferior in quality. He wrote for the

57 Rapallo, where Sibelius composed his Second Symphony

58, 59 (opposite)
Sibelius's villa
at Järvenpää

keyboard throughout his life, but many of the pieces, particularly the ones written during the 1914–18 war, are in the nature of pot-boilers. Although he played the piano (and indeed is often pictured doing so), he had no feeling for the idiom, and confessed as much to Walter Legge: 'I dislike the piano: it is an unsatisfactory, ungrateful instrument, an instrument for which only one composer, Chopin, has succeeded in writing perfectly, and of which only two others, Debussy and Schumann, have had an intimate understanding.' With rare exceptions, his most characteristic thoughts did not find their way into his piano music. In this respect he may be said to resemble Berlioz, whose lack of interest

Overleaf: 60   The English critic Rosa Newmarch, one of Sibelius's keenest admirers.
61   Sir Granville Bantock, to whom Sibelius dedicated the Third Symphony

à mon bien cher et honoré ami Jean Sibelius

Rosa Newmarch

61

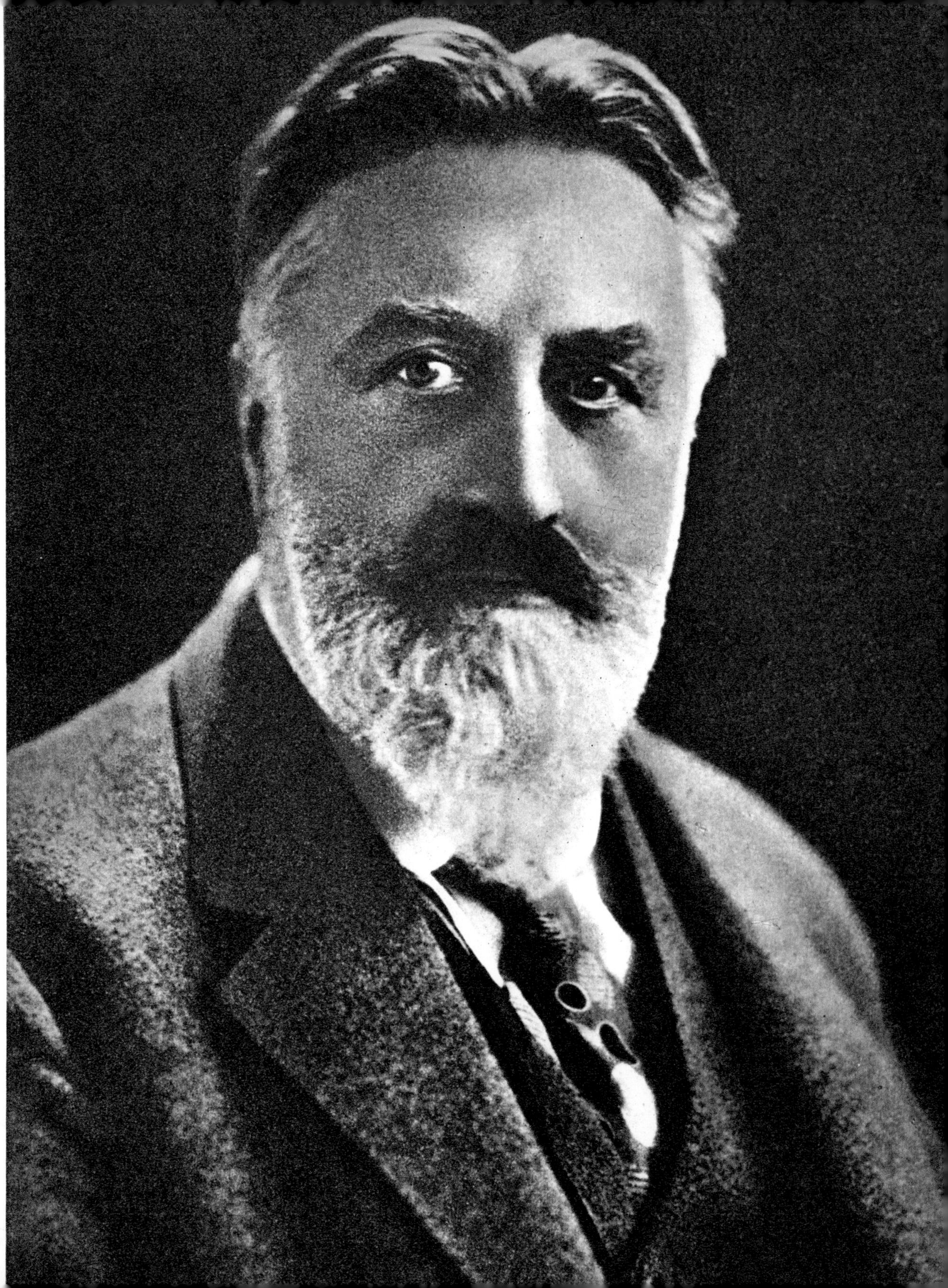

in the piano went further still, in that he hardly wrote for the keyboard at all.

To return to the Fourth Symphony, its most striking feature, its real point of divergence from current practice, was the quality of its orchestral writing. In terms of the conventional post-romantic orchestral sound, or even the impressionistic orchestral palette of Debussy, this is a highly novel score. To call it 'chamber-like' – Harold Johnson's phrase – is an oversimplification, though an understandable one. Sibelius does achieve something of the economy and intimacy of chamber music, but the instrumentation is always essentially orchestral. (Incidentally, it may well have started life as a string quartet, as Johnson suggests.) If the Fourth Symphony met with general bewilderment both in Scandinavia and abroad (it was denounced in Boston as an assembly of 'dissonant, doleful mutterings, generally leading nowhere'), it also acquired some staunch supporters. Among them was Toscanini, who, characteristically, reacted to its hostile reception by immediately billing it for repeat. ,

When Sibelius had gone to Breitkopf in 1898, he had anticipated that his chief following would be in Germany and German-speaking Europe, but it gradually became evident that his music was becoming extremely popular with Anglo-Saxon audiences. He had visited England in 1908 to conduct the first English performance of the Third Symphony, and he returned the following year to direct the revised version of *En Saga*. It was on this occasion that he heard music by Bax, whom he met, and Elgar's First Symphony. He also met Debussy and d'Indy during this trip, and finished work on *Voces intimae,* his only mature string quartet and one of the purest of his compositions. Because of his illness he had to forgo alcohol and cigars, a considerable sacrifice for such a *bon viveur,* and those who met him, among them Goossens, reported that he was not the merriest of companions. (His wife once described this period of self-denial as 'the quiet years'.) He went on from London to Paris and Berlin, and altogether did a lot of travelling at this time. There were concert tours in Sweden and the Baltic States in 1911, and later in the same year he went back both to Paris and to Berlin, where he heard a good deal of new music.

In 1912 he paid yet another visit to England, to conduct the Fourth Symphony at Birmingham, and during his stay was commissioned by the Gloucester Festival to write a new choral and orchestral work. This piece never materialized: 'So far,' he told Rosa Newmarch, 'I have no inspiration to write [a choral work], and cannot, will not, force myself.' Instead, he decided to offer Gloucester another work, *Luonnotar,* which

Anglo-Saxon following

67

63 Mahler, whom Sibelius met in Helsinki in 1907

had probably been written a year or so earlier, but had not yet been performed. This tone-poem for soprano and orchestra, which tells the story of the world's creation as related in the *Kalevala,* is one of Sibelius's most haunting, original and beautiful compositions. Aino Ackté, for whom he wrote it, was a singer with a remarkably wide tessitura, and the work's neglect is due partly to the cruelly demanding vocal writing that her virtuosity inspired.

England was not alone in its response to Sibelius. The Vienna Conservatoire offered him a chair of composition in 1912 (which he declined), and he now had a strong following in the United States. Indeed, the Third Symphony was given its American première before its English, and the Violin Concerto was heard in a large number of American musical centres only a year after the Berlin première under Strauss. He declined an invitation to conduct in New York in 1913, but the following year he accepted an invitation to go to Norfolk, Connecticut, to conduct a specially commissioned work at a festival there.

The invitation, which came from a rich American patron of music, Carl Stoeckel, arrived at the same time as an offer from the University of Yale of an honorary doctorate. Perhaps it was this double offer that persuaded him to make the trip. In any event, he arrived in New York in May 1914, to be met by Stoeckel and the press. He told Ekman afterwards: 'I was quite astonished at being so well-known in America. I should never have believed it.' He was completely overwhelmed by Stoeckel's generosity and the lavishness of his entertainment. 'I was surrounded with everything that the luxury of the American upper classes had to offer. I have never, before or after, lived such a wonderful life. I recall with special regret the cigars that Mr Stoeckel provided me with, which I dared not touch for fear of a renewed infection of the throat. What a fool I was at that time!' The orchestra Sibelius was to conduct was handpicked from among the finest players in Boston and New York, and he was delighted by its response to his direction. The concert at which he gave *The Oceanides,* the newly composed piece, also included *Finlandia, Pohjola's Daughter,* and the *King Christian II* suite; all told, he conducted nine of his works at the Norfolk festival.

The Oceanides is almost the only one of Sibelius's tone-poems not to have been inspired by Finnish mythology. Indeed, with its Homeric inspiration (the Oceanides being the ocean nymphs of Greek mythology), it is at times almost Mediterranean in feeling. To judge by his letters to his brother Christian, he was particularly pleased with this work – as well he might be, for it is a powerful and evocative piece of composition.

Many commentators have followed Gray in speaking of its 'pointillisme' and impressionism, but in fact, in its essential processes, it does not depart from Sibelius's normal ways of thought. The orchestration, with the delicate writing for wind and strings and the liquid sounds from the harp, goes further than most of his tone-poems in direct pictorialism, and since the musical imagery, particularly towards the end, is strongly suggestive of the ebb and flow of the sea, it is hardly surprising that Debussy, the greatest poet of the sea, should come to mind. Before leaving America, Sibelius presented Stoeckel with the autograph score of the work (he subsequently revised it, though it never underwent so drastic a change as the Fifth Symphony). It was on his way back to Europe that the news of the assassination at Sarajevo broke.

The war years The war had two practical effects on Sibelius's life. First, when Russia entered the conflict against Germany, Sibelius was immediately cut off from a major source of revenue, for although his state grant had been increased at the time he turned down the offer from Vienna, it was still not sufficient to meet his needs. As far as Breitkopf was concerned, he was an enemy alien, and since Finland did not belong to the Berne Convention, he derived no benefit from foreign performances. In due course he got round the difficulty, by making arrangements with the Danish publisher Hansen, and he also found an English publisher, but this was only later. Technically, Sibelius was a Russian citizen, and Ekman tells us how in 1914 he had to withdraw from a concert in Malmö because he insisted on being billed as a Finnish composer and the authorities would not do this for fear of incurring Russian displeasure. To offset the loss of income from Breitkopf and Härtel, he began to produce a large quantity of trifling pieces for piano, and violin and piano, songs and the like, aimed at the home market. Some of these, like the E minor violin sonatina, have distinct artistic merit, but others are quite simply pieces of unblushing jobbery. The second effect of the war was to limit his travelling. Ever since he had established his reputation abroad, Sibelius had been travelling widely: apart from visits to England, America and, above all, Italy, he was a frequent visitor to Berlin, Vienna and St Petersburg. Naturally, he was affected by being cut off from the stimulus they provided. Above all, he missed being able to conduct (and hear) the great international orchestras.

But to say that Sibelius was entirely cut off from abroad is not wholly true: he undertook a Scandinavian tour in both 1915 and 1916. Nor is it entirely fair to say that he produced only trifles. The Fifth Symphony, after all, belongs to these years, and, of the shorter pieces, the two sets of

Humoresques for violin and orchestra are far from trifling. They contain a charm, a wealth of feeling and a sheer quality of invention that put them into a category of their own. They have the requisite lightness of touch and yet are tinged with a nostalgia and poetry that cannot be too highly prized. As for the Fifth Symphony, it first began to take shape in his mind a month or so after the outbreak of war, and it was completed in time for performance on his fiftieth birthday on 8 December 1915. In the Scandinavian countries the celebrations surrounding this day in one's life are both extensive and exhausting: they tend to exceed those of any other day, even one's wedding day, in lavishness. Sibelius's birthday, which was celebrated as a national holiday, culminated in this première of the new symphony under the composer's own baton.

Although in its final version the Fifth is one of Sibelius's most popular works, it appears in its initial stages to have given him more trouble than any other of his symphonies. At its first performance, the composer's first biographer, Erik Furuhjelm, who had prepared his biography almost as a kind of one-man *Festschrift* for the occasion, recalls that the work was in four movements; yet, as we all know, the final version is in three. Immediately after its première, at which, incidentally, he conducted *The Oceanides* and the two Serenades for violin and orchestra as well, he withdrew it for revision and presented a new, 'definitive' version the following year. In this, the first two movements were linked together; but after only two performances, in Helsinki and Turku, he withdrew the work yet again. The symphony announced in 1916 as being in its 'definitive' form underwent further changes, and in a letter of 1918 he describes it as having four movements: the first 'entirely new', the second based on the old second movement, the third based on the end of the old first movement and the last based on the old motives but 'stronger in revision'.

So many writers have puzzled over the evolution of the final version of the first movement, completed in 1919, that it is worth noting these changes. The final first movement does, in fact, represent a conflation of the first two movements, so perfectly integrated that one is tempted to hail the result as Sibelius's most original sonata-movement. In sheer heroic sweep the finale of the Fifth offers a degree of physical exhilaration and a sustained flow of energy that none of its predecessors quite matches, even if the finale of the Third comes very near to it. A parallel with the Third also arises in the slow movement, which acts as a foil to the two powerful outer movements. In both symphonies, the slow movement is predominantly sunny and relaxed in character, though in that of the

71

Fifth there is evidence of controlled power when the texture darkens.

For all his labours with the Fifth Symphony and the quantity of other music that occupied him during the war years, Sibelius, like everyone else, was drawn into the tragedy that overtook Finland after the October Revolution in 1917. Shortly after the February uprising that brought Kerensky's provisional government to power, the Finnish middle classes began to organize themselves into para-military units, ostensibly to defend themselves against the possibility of disaffected Russian soldiers getting out of hand, but also to provide against the danger of a similar working-class uprising in Finland itself. The Social Democrats and the Communist sympathizers did the same, and the rival groups became known as White and Red Guards respectively. A month or so after the October Revolution, the Finnish parliament declared the country independent, and at the end of January 1918 a left-wing *coup* placed the Reds in power in Helsinki and its environs, and unleashed a bitter civil war.

Sibelius's sympathies had always been anti-Russian, and in this struggle he was pro-White. Järvenpää, where he had his villa Ainola, was in a Red-controlled area; the local Red Guards forbade him to leave the house, which they twice subjected to a thorough search, and generally adopted a threatening attitude. Had they known that he had anonymously written a march for a batallion of Finnish volunteers who had served with the Germans on the Russian front and who were technically rebels apart from being Whites, they would doubtless have shot him out of hand. However, Kajanus managed to persuade the Red commandant to allow him to come to Helsinki, where there was greater discipline among the Reds and less haphazard violence. So Sibelius left his home and joined his brother Christian in the capital. This was a period when the whole family suffered great privation. A few weeks

later, Mannerheim, who commanded the Whites with the support of ten thousand German troops, occupied Helsinki; and, a few months after that, the Armistice of November 1918 was agreed, and hostilities brought to an end.

Immediate post-war years

With the end of the war, normal musical life was slowly restored, and Sibelius threw himself into his work once more. His ideas for the Sixth and Seventh Symphonies had begun to take shape already in the turbulent spring of 1918, and although they were still to change a good deal, they were now developing. A large quantity of choral music of an occasional nature, as well as much light music, such as the *Valse lyrique,* some piano music and a patriotic cantata, *Our Native Land (Oma maa),* occupied the immediate post-war years. Also, to his delight, he began again to travel. In 1919 he attended the Nordic Music Festival in Copenhagen, at which he conducted his Second Symphony with great success. Concert tours were planned again, and he was even invited to become the first director of the newly founded Eastman School of Music in America. This he at first accepted, after insisting on a salary of $20,000, but later decided against it. Apart from the fact that he would have had to uproot himself – in his early fifties – from his native country, he was never much interested in teaching.

In 1921, Sibelius was invited to conduct a series of concerts in England, where he was reunited with his old friend Busoni. Busoni played his own *Indian Fantasy* and a Mozart concerto, and Sibelius conducted his Fourth Symphony. Sir Henry Wood, in his memoirs, recounts the difficulties of keeping track of the two of them: 'I could generally manage Busoni when I had him to myself. But my heart was always in my mouth if he met Sibelius. I never knew where they would get to. They would forget the time of the concert at which they were to appear; they hardly knew the day of the week. One year I was directing the Birmingham Festival and had to commission a friend never to let these two out of his sight. He had quite an exciting time for two or three days, following them around from restaurant to restaurant. He told me he never knew what time they went to bed or got up in the morning. They were like a couple of irresponsible schoolboys.'

The Sixth Symphony

Despite the great output of trivia (the two suites, *Suite mignonne* and *Suite champêtre,* are examples), work was progressing on the Sixth, the Seventh and possibly on an eighth symphony. In a letter to a friend, Sibelius describes the Sixth Symphony as being 'wild and impassioned in character. Sombre, with pastoral contrasts. Probably in four movements, with the end rising to a sombre roaring of the orchestra in which

66   A letter from Busoni to Sibelius, dated 29 October 1912, in which Busoni asks for the score of *Historical Scenes*. The letter ends: 'I'll play for you this evening as well as I am able' – a reference to the concert he was giving that night

Grand Hôtel
FENNIA
(HELSINGFORS)

Telefoner:
KONTOR 47 31
ETTER & RESANDERUM
21, 48 03, 50 10.
KAFÉ 71 06

Lieber Jean
Sibelius, ich
bin ausserordentlich inter-
essiert, deine historischen
Bilder zu kennen, möchte
sie gerne auf die Reise mit-
nehmen und frage deshalb
ganz unbescheiden an,
ob ich sie von Dir bekommen
kann. — ? — Ich werde
heute Abend für Dich
spielen, so gut ich vermag.
        Tausend Grüsse.
            Dein Freund
29 Okt. 1912. Ferruccio Busoni

the main theme is drowned.' The symphony itself hardly corresponds to the description 'wild and impassioned': it is, on the contrary, serene, and its quietist nature often eludes the interpreter. The composer himself conducted the first performance in February 1923, in an all-Sibelius programme which included the *Scène autrefois* and the *Suite champêtre*.

The Sixth has never been the most popular of the seven symphonies, but it has excited the admiration of connoisseurs of the composer. Like the Fourth, this is *echt* Sibelius; Ralph Wood called it his greatest symphony, 'a dazzling display of a technique so personal and so assured that its very achievements are hidden in its mastery and in its entire synthesis with its subject matter.' Simon Parmet, the Finnish conductor and writer, spoke of it as 'the stepchild among the symphonies, neglected by many but loved by those who are attached to its simple, barren beauty.' It was this work that occasioned Sibelius's famous remark that while other composers were offering the public 'cocktails of various hues, I offer pure spring water'. And, indeed, compared with the opulent orchestral textures and highly spiced harmonies that Strauss, Ravel, Stravinsky and others were employing, Sibelius's symphony seems unusually pure, concentrating on inner essentials without any disposition towards display. Like the First Symphony, the Sixth uses a harp, the only other Sibelius symphony to do so; otherwise, it is scored for relatively modest forces, double woodwind, four horns, three trumpets, and trombones, timpani and strings. The modal flavour of the work has prompted some comment, inspired largely by Cecil Gray's pioneering book in the 1930s, but in fact this quality is present in much of Sibelius's music from the *Karelia* suite onwards. It is more prominent in the Sixth, because the restraint of the orchestration and the polyphonic nature of the writing serve to underline the modal impact, as well as to remind the listener of Sibelius's admiration for the great Renaissance polyphonists, Lassus, Palestrina and the composers of the English school.

The Seventh Symphony

The Seventh Symphony followed the Sixth after a gap of only a year. It proved once again the truth of the statement that Sibelius never approaches the symphonic problem in the same way. Each of the symphonies shows a continuing search for new formal means: there is no stereotyped mould into which ideas are poured; yet at the same time the listener is never made to feel aware of experimentation with form. The ideas of each of the seven symphonies dictate the flow of the music that follows, and each sets up its own disciplinary logic which is scrupulously observed to the end. Unlike any of Sibelius's other symphonies, the Seventh is in one continuous movement; and, unlike any

76

previous attempt at writing a one-movement symphony, the work emphatically does not sound like four separate movements played without a break. Admittedly, there are passages that have the character of a scherzo or of a slow section, but it is quite impossible to say where one section ends and another begins, so complete is Sibelius's mastery of transition and control of simultaneous tempi. It is, in fact, the climax of a lifetime's work in this particular field; like the first movement of the Fifth Symphony, one thinks of it as a constantly growing entity, in which the thematic metamorphosis works at such a level of sophistication that the listener is barely aware of it.

When the work first appeared, it was billed as *Fantasia Sinfonica*. Sibelius himself conducted its first performance, which took place in Stockholm in March 1924, together with the First Symphony and the Violin Concerto. Later, when it was published, Sibelius called it the Seventh Symphony – and rightly so, for no work more clearly embodies the essence of organic symphonic thinking. To define its structure or demarcate its growth is impossible, for it unfolds in an astonishingly subtle manner. All the material of the symphony is in some way or other derived from the ideas which are stated before the first appearance of the majestic trombone theme. This, incidentally, is heard three times during the course of the work, and on each occasion it emerges with greater strength and nobility. After its first appearance, the music changes direction, albeit subtly, the tempo quickens and the music assumes the character of a scherzo; after its second appearance, the tension relaxes and there is an intermezzo-like section; and finally, with the third appearance of the theme, we reach the most powerful and impressive climax of all.

In its degree of organic integration and the subtlety of its thematic metamorphosis, the Seventh stands right at the peak of the symphonic tradition. Oddly enough, it was Finland in this instance that was slow in responding to it. Its first Finnish performance did not take place until three years after it was heard in Stockholm, by which time both Stokowski and Koussevitzky had conducted it in America.

In 1925 Sibelius celebrated his sixtieth birthday. Tributes, telegrams, flowers and other gifts were showered upon him in even greater profusion than had been possible on his fiftieth, held in the middle of the Great War. The Finnish government increased his pension, there was a nation-wide fund in his honour which reached a total of 150,000 Finnish marks, and his publisher, Hansen, gave him a handsome sum in addition. Most of 1925 was devoted to composing the incidental music for a lavish production of Shakespeare's *Tempest,* which was scheduled for performance in Copenhagen in spring 1926. The Royal Theatre, Copenhagen, serves in the capacity both of a theatre and of an opera house: hence, the orchestra available to him was a large one. The *Tempest* music contains much of Sibelius's most atmospheric and powerful theatre music, and it is a pity that the adverse opinions of such writers as Ralph Wood, whose excellent judgment escaped him on this occasion, has discouraged its performance. The Prelude is certainly among the most effective examples of storm music in the entire orchestral repertoire, and it is difficult to imagine more hauntingly poetic or beautiful miniatures than the *Oak Tree,* the *Berceuse* and the *Chorus of the Winds.*

Tapiola   As soon as the *Tempest* music was finished, Sibelius left Finland for his beloved Italy, and it is ironic to think that the most fiercely Nordic of all his compositions, *Tapiola,* was conceived in the relaxed surroundings of the Mediterranean. This profoundly original work, commissioned by Walter Damrosch for performance by the New York Philharmonic Society, proved to be the last major work that Sibelius wrote, and in a sense it is the most uncompromising of all.

After the First World War the symphonic poem seemed to be going out of fashion: Strauss had begun to turn from the tone-poem to the opera already at the end of the nineteenth century, and Sibelius himself had written nothing in this form since *The Oceanides* (1914). *Tapiola* is a work that has excited the greatest enthusiasm among Sibelius's admirers, Cecil Gray claiming that 'even if Sibelius had written nothing else, [it] would entitle him to a place amongst the greatest masters of all time.' Many have argued that it is symphonic and, in the sense that there is an extraordinary degree of organic integration, this is so. However, the usual contrast of key centres is absent, for the whole work is anchored in B minor, and the piece is wholly monothematic.

Commenting on this absence of movement and contrasting it with the procedure of the Seventh Symphony, Robert Simpson wrote: 'The symphony is like a great planet in orbit, its movements vast, inexorable, seemingly imperceptible to its inhabitants. But, you may object, the Finnish forests of *Tapiola* are also on the surface of such a planet, revolving. Yes, but we never leave them, we are filled with *expectation* and nothing but a great wind arises. There is no real sense of movement. The symphony has both the cosmic motion of the earth and the teeming activity that is upon it: we are made to observe one or the other at the composer's will. Indeed, observe is not the right word – we experience

78

Kirjallisuutta ja taidetta.

~~~

Jean Sibelius Amerikassa.

Suurenmoinen menestys.

Vihitty musiikintohtoriksi Yalen yliopistossa. — Lähtenyt paluumatkalle eilen.

Jean Sibelius saapui New Yorkiin toukokuun 27 p:nä.

Jo matkan warrella saapui Kaiser Wilhelm 2:seen useita langattomia sähkösanomia, joissa Amerikan säweltäjät ja muut sikäläisissä musiikkipiireissä tunnetut henkilöt lausuiwat Sibeliuksen terwetulleeksi Amerikaan. Wastaanotto New Yorkissa oli erittäin sydämellinen. T. k. 4 p:nä oli suuri konsertti miljonääri Stoeckelin Norfolkissa sijaitsewalle maatilalle rakennetussa isossa konserttisalissa 3,000 amerikalaisen ja europalaisen wieraan läsnäollessa. Menestys oli suurenmoinen. Amerikan suurimmat musiikkimiehet ja huomattawimmat arwostelijat oliwat läsnä. Orkesteriin kuului 86 henkeä. Ohjelmassa oliwat seuraawat numerot: Pohjolan tytär, Kung Kristian-swiitti, Tuonelan joutsen, Walse triste, Finlandia ja „Aallottaret", jonka wiimemainitun kappaleen hra Stoeckel oli erikoisesti säweltäjältä tilannut tätä tilaisuutta warten.

Painetun ohjelman lopussa oli Maamme-laulu englannin kielellä ja kehoitettiin yleisöä sen esittämisen aikana nousemaan seisoalleen ja ottamaan osaa lauluun. Yleisö kunnioitti Sibeliusta nousemalla seisoalleen, kun hän astui esille johtamaan säwellyksiänsä.

Keskiwiikkona t. k. 17 pnä kunnioit-

---

these extremes and when one is operative, the other does not exist for us' (*Sibelius and Nielsen*, London 1965).

It is true that in *Tapiola* Sibelius achieved a degree of identification with nature that is more complete than in any of his other works; it is comparable only with Debussy's achievement in *Nuages* and *La Mer*. Never before had Sibelius evoked the terror of the unending, sunless forests so powerfully, even if, towards the close, there is a longing for human contact. Certainly no composer before him had drawn sounds from the orchestra like these: it is an entirely new world. After *Tapiola's* completion, Sibelius's publisher asked him for a line of explanation on the title (Tapio being the God of the Forest in Finnish mythology), and this prompted the following quatrain:

> *Widespread they stand, the Northland's dusky forests,*
> *Ancient, mysterious, brooding savage dreams;*
> *Within them dwells the Forest's mighty god,*
> *And wood-sprites in the gloom, weave magic secrets.*

The silence

Tapiola stands as a crowning achievement, and one can well imagine the eager anticipation with which the musical world awaited Sibelius's next work. But no new work followed. Although an eighth symphony had been promised to a number of conductors, it never materialized. In June 1932, this symphony was even announced for publication in the brochure of the HMV Sibelius Society. Later in the same year it was promised to Koussevitzky as a climax to the cycle of symphonies he was presenting in Boston, and a similar promise was made to Beecham. Many years later Sibelius told Basil Cameron that he had completed the work several times and was not satisfied with it. Cameron was not the only visitor who saw a score. There is no doubt that an eighth symphony was either completed or near completion at some point during the early 1930s. According to one rumour, the score was actually delivered to a copyist; according to another, it was

69   A report in the Finnish press of Sibelius's arrival in New York

actually put into rehearsal. In short, it is difficult to disentangle legend from reality where this work is concerned. What is certain is that Sibelius's persistent doubts led him to parry questions by saying that the symphony would be released after his death.

Sibelius's reticence over the legendary symphony was not, of course, an isolated case. He had been similarly reluctant to release for performance or publication earlier work which he felt might damage his standing. The early string quartet, op. 4, never appeared in print, and only a movement from it was performed in the 1930s; his hesitation over the two 'Lemminkäinen' Legends has already been noted; and even the 'Kullervo' Symphony, the work which established him in Finland, he forbade to be played, so that it had to wait until 1958 for a full-scale performance.

Although it was said that Sibelius was still composing, the last three decades of his life were as unproductive as his life itself was uneventful. He was to have accompanied the Finnish National Orchestra on its London visit in 1934, and again a visit was promised for the 1938 festival conducted by Beecham; but he did not come on either occasion. In fact, from the 1930s onwards, he gave up travelling altogether, and spent his remaining years at Järvenpää as quietly as he could. In 1939 he conducted his *Andante festivo* (a small piece dating from the early 1920s) for a short-wave transmission for the New York World Fair, but apart from this his withdrawal from activity was almost complete. He continued to receive a constant stream of visitors from the Anglo-Saxon countries, though as time wore on these became a source of worry to him and were not encouraged.

Sibelius's reputation grew apace, and literature on him began to swell. Rosa Newmarch had published a pioneering pamphlet as early as 1906, and the first full-scale biography, by Erik Furuhjelm, had appeared on his fiftieth birthday, in 1915. The Finnish writer Karl Ekman, whose mother, the singer Ida Ekman, was a distinguished interpreter of Sibelius's songs, wrote an official biography in the mid-1930s and another of his countrymen, Bengt de Törne, followed suit. But the most influential book on the composer was undoubtedly Cecil Gray's monograph, which made its appearance in 1931.

In his autobiography, *Musical Chairs,* Gray gives a vivid picture of his first meeting with Sibelius, in Finland in 1929. At first their conversation floundered in a mixture of French and German; Gray describes their exchanges as 'strained'. However, at some point he must have made a remark that pleased Sibelius: 'He suddenly exclaimed, "But, Mr Gray,

Critical standing

81

Praeses et Socii

UNIVERSITATIS YALENSIS

In Novo Portu in Republica Connecticutensi.

Omnibus ad quos hae litterae pervenant

Salutem.

Vobis illud notum sit, nos   *Jean Sibelius*

qui aures nostras carminibus suavibus oblectavit

Musicae Doctoris   titulo adornavisse atque

auxisse, eique fruenda dedisse omnia jura, honores, insignia quae apud

nos ad Gradum Doctoralem   evectis concedi soleant.

In cujus rei testimonium et Praesidis et Scribae Academici

manum et Universitatis signum huic documento apponenda

curavimus, ante diem quintadecima Kalendas Quintiles Anno Domini

MCMXIV.

Scriba.   Praeses.

you are not a journalist – you are a musician! Why did you not say so at the start?" He became a different man, jumped up, shook hands with me warmly, produced a bottle of whisky from the cupboard, and from that moment onwards all went well. When we parted, it was arranged that I should lunch with him the next day at the hotel where he always stayed on his visits to the Finnish capital. Not only did he prove to be the perfect host in all that pertains to the table, but the intellectual feast he spreads before his guests is even more magnificent. Of himself and his work he speaks diffidently and unwillingly. One quickly realizes that he prefers to discuss any and every subject on earth – literature, philosophy, painting, politics, science. Suddenly, on looking round the restaurant, I noticed that we were the only people present and, glancing at my watch, discovered that it was about six o'clock. Murmuring a few words of apology for having outstayed my welcome, I made as if

71 Sibelius (fourth from the right) in the degree procession

Overleaf: 72 Ainola, in the exceptionally severe winter of 1917.
73 Aino Sibelius

◀ 70 The honorary doctorate from Yale University

to depart; but my host appeared mildly surprised at this suggestion, and prevailed upon me to stay for dinner, which we duly consumed at the same table. We did not separate until seven o'clock in the morning.'

Gray's championship, along with that of Newman, and in the United States Olin Downes, did much to advance Sibelius as the leading composer of the day. Gray's monograph, together with the brilliantly written *Music Ho!* (1934) by the composer-conductor Constant Lambert, created the climate for the boom in Sibelius that took place in the Anglo-Saxon countries in the 1930s. In Lambert's book, subtitled 'A Study of Music in Decline', Stravinsky and Schoenberg were lambasted in no uncertain terms, while Sibelius was singled out for the highest praise:

75   Sibelius at Ainola

87

◀ 74   Sibelius with his two youngest children, Heidi and Margareta

76　In Capri, early 1920s

'One is so used to being told that some trifling, short-winded, neo-classical pastiche represents a return to the spirit of Bach that one is a little chary of evoking the shade of Beethoven where Sibelius is concerned; but the comparison is inevitable, for not only is Sibelius the most important symphonic writer since Beethoven, but he may even be described as the only writer since Beethoven who has definitely advanced what, after all, is the most complete formal expression of the musical spirit.' Admittedly, Gray and Lambert were the most ardent of the admirers of Sibelius's music, but there were others, notably the distinguished musical analyst Donald Tovey, who recognized the quality of his achievement. By contrast, neither Germany nor France could muster so solid or powerful a core of scholars, critics and writers to champion Sibelius's cause.

It would, of course, be absurd to attribute to any critical body too great a hand in Sibelius's popularity. Concert promoters, and recording executives like Walter Legge who pioneered the HMV Sibelius Society, made an important contribution; but the most influential of Sibelius's advocates were the conductors, not only Koussevitzky, Beecham and Sir Henry Wood, but also less well-known figures such as Clarence Raybould and Basil Cameron. So firmly was Sibelius's fame established by this time that, at one poll of concert-goers in the United States, he outstripped in popularity all other composers, including Beethoven, Mozart and even Tchaikovsky.

Sibelius's popularity varied from country to country for reasons that are perhaps more nationalistic than musical. Thus, in England, for the greater part of the nineteenth century, musical ideas were entirely dominated by the German tradition, and English composers produced pale, academic reflections of Mendelssohn and Brahms. The first sign of a change came with the wave of interest in the Russian nationalists, notably Scriabin, in the early decades of the present century. This was followed by a general widening of the horizon and deepening of perspective in English musical taste. There was a more ready interest in new music from France, and a growing awareness of the important legacy of Tudor and seventeenth-century music and the folk song of the British Isles. In short, there developed a tendency among musicians and listeners to reject the dominance of the German masters and the whole Central European tradition. This tendency explains why much Central European music, such as Mahler's, took decades to gain acceptance in the English-speaking world: the music of Richard Strauss is the sole exception.

In France and Germany, different factors applied. France, with her strong and self-sufficient traditions, has never shown the same receptivity to new musical ideas as have countries which lack such traditions. The French remained indifferent to Sibelius in the 1930s, just as they remained indifferent to much else, including Brahms and Mahler. German interest, though greater, was again not comparable with that of the English-speaking countries, and was complicated by nationalism; just as England rebelled against the Austro-German hegemony in music, the musical establishment in Berlin and Vienna was reluctant to accept the idea of a major composer working outside the central tradition. Interest in Elgar, which had been so great in Germany before the war, stopped after 1914, and Sibelius suffered much the same fate. Breitkopf and Härtel were no longer so active on his behalf; there were relatively few attempts to break down the natural conservatism and insularity of the German public, reinforced as it was by defeat and disillusion.

The outbreak of the Second World War in the autumn of 1939, and the Soviet Union's attack on Finland in November, marked the start of a period of great privation for Finland. Sibelius's name was invoked in appeals to the American people for help (a stamp with his head and the words 'I need your help' was issued to raise funds for the Finnish cause), and his music once again served patriotic ends. In 1940 an armistice was agreed, and Finland was forced to surrender parts of Karelia and northern Finland. When in the following year Hitler attacked Russia, Finland entered the war as a co-belligerent to reclaim her losses, and Sibelius unwillingly joined the formidable list of composers, including Bruckner and Wagner, whose names were invoked by the Nazis. Unlike Shostakovich, whose symphonies were mobilized to serve the Allied cause, Sibelius was in the unusual situation of enjoying popularity with friend and foe alike, although it is only fair to add that the Allies, recognizing Finland's special position, were never formally at war with her.

The last years   These years brought enormous suffering to Finland, particularly when she endeavoured to extricate herself from the German alliance. In April 1945, *The Times* reported that Sibelius was in need (the report was subsequently denied), and it is a measure of the affection and respect in which he was held that the public response was immediate both in England and in America. And this hold over the public persisted right through the 1940s. (In England alone, the symphonies appeared regularly at the annual Promenade Concerts, and Sibelius's work was rarely absent from broadcast programmes.)

Above all, Sibelius was a national figure, perhaps to a greater extent

90

77 Busoni and Sibelius in London, 1921

78   At the Nordic Music Festival, Copenhagen, summer 1919. From left to right: Frederik Schnedler-Petersen, Robert Kajanus, Jean Sibelius, Georg Høeberg, Erkki Melartin, Wilhelm Stenhammar, Carl Nielsen and Johan Halvorsen

than any earlier composer, not excluding Chopin or Dvořák. Through the medium of his work people first became aware of Finland, a remote province on the northern borders of Tsarist Russia. His birthdays were national events, and on his eighty-fifth, in 1950, the President of Finland motored out to Järvenpää to pay the nation's respects. On his ninetieth he received more than twelve hundred telegrams, cigars from Sir Winston Churchill, tapes from Toscanini, and an enormous number of other presents and letters. Arrangements were made for him to hear his ninetieth-birthday concert, given by Sir Thomas Beecham in London and beamed on a specially powerful signal so that he could receive it at Järvenpää. The extent of his fame was such that not only was the con-

79   The Sibelius family, 1923

servatoire, or Musikinstitut, at which he had studied named after him, but several parks and more than fifty streets, one as far away as Jamaica.

Sibelius was remarkably long-lived by any standards. For one who during his youth had enjoyed indifferent health (Aino Sibelius was warned that she would be nursing an invalid when she married him) and whose life was seriously threatened at the height of his powers, the great age he attained seems incredible. His death came in his ninety-second year, on 20 September 1957, when he suffered a cerebral haemorrhage. He had spent a normal morning, having read the papers and taken lunch as usual. He collapsed in the early afternoon and lost consciousness at about four o'clock. He died in the evening, as, incidentally, the Helsinki

93

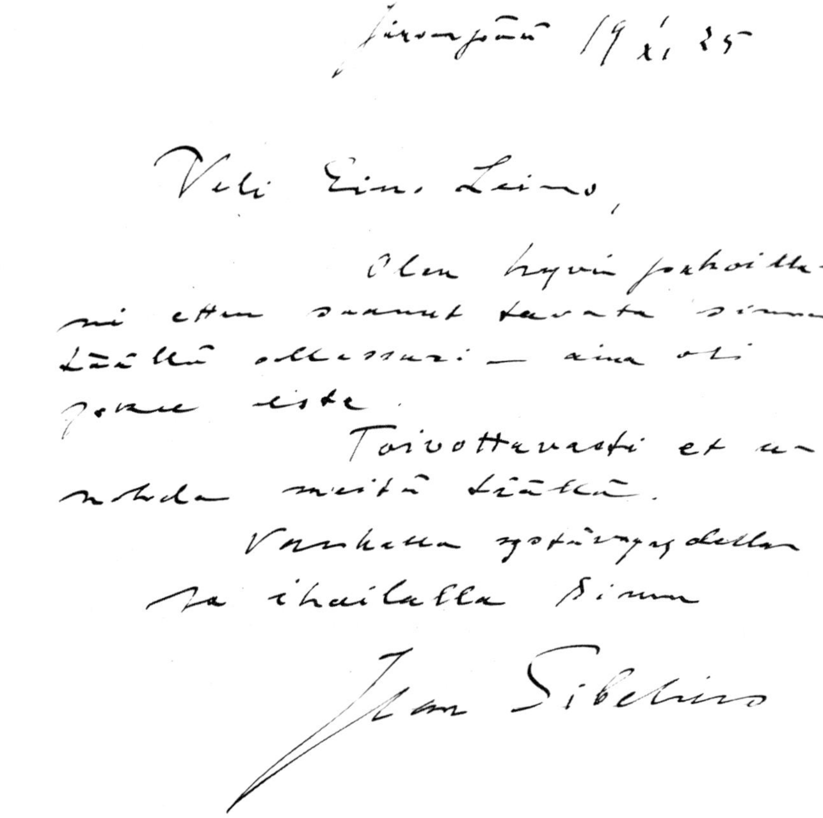

Järvenpää 19.xi.35

Veli Eino Leino,

Olen hyvin pahoillani että saanut tavata sinua täällä ollessasi — aina oli jokin este.

Toivottavasti ett' en nähdä meitä täällä.

Vanhalla ystävyydellä ja ihailulla Sinun

Jean Sibelius

80 A letter to Eino Leino

Orchestra under Sir Malcolm Sargent were giving the Fifth Symphony. He received a state funeral in the cathedral, the Storkyrkan, and the service included *In Memoriam,* the slow movement of the Fourth Symphony, *The Swan of Tuonela* and the *Andante festivo.* He was buried in the grounds of Ainola, his villa at Järvenpää, where he had spent more than fifty years of his life.

The inevitable reaction against Sibelius's dominance set in during the mid-1950s. The slackening of critical interest in his work is reflected in the comparative paucity of the literature. After 1947, the year in which Gerald Abraham's book on Sibelius was published, the only two studies of him to appear in English were a translation of Parmet's book on the symphonies and an American biography that illustrated the trend in some quarters to 'cut him down to size'. This was the critical reaction. The same could well have happened as regards the reaction of

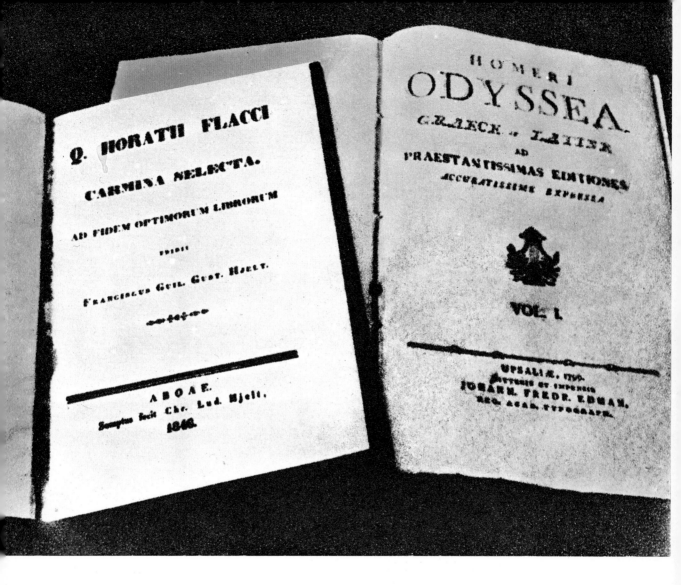

the general public, with whom many great composers – Telemann, Vivaldi, Bach – have lost favour after their death. In Sibelius's case, however, there was a new factor: the role of the gramophone. Sibelius and Elgar are the first two composers whose reputations have been very largely governed, from the outset, by the availability of gramophone records of their music. In Elgar's case the gramophone has given us the composer's own interpretations of most of his works; whereas in Sibelius's case it has been the means of expressing the public reaction, as opposed to the critical reaction, to his art. Throughout the 1950s and

81 Two books from Sibelius's library. He was especially fond of the classics

95

◀ 82   Sibelius in 1934

83, 84   Sibelius arriving
for his 70th birthday
celebrations, 1935. Below,
His 70th birthday concert.
The photograph shows
three Finnish Presidents:
Relander (left), Ståhlberg
and Mannerheim

Overleaf:
85   Title-page of *Finlandia*.
86   Sibelius in old age

JEAN SIBELIUS

FINLANDIA

TONDICHTUNG FÜR ORCHESTER

OP. 26 NR. 7

BEARBEITUNG
FÜR PIANOFORTE ZU 2 HÄNDEN

With best wishes to the Mayor
New York, Mr. Vincent Impellitteri

Jean Sibelius

1952

Eigentum der Verleger für alle Länder

BREITKOPF & HÄRTEL
LEIPZIG

Für Finnland:
O.Y. Fazerin Musiikkikauppa, Helsinki.
A.B. Fazers Musikhandel, Helsingfors.

87   Walking in the forest

88   Sibelius with a ▶
       Bach score

90　In his old age, Sibelius permitted himself once more the occasional cigar

early 1960s, his reputation in critical circles in both England and the United States was at its lowest ebb; concert performances were comparatively scarce, and new admirers of his music had yet to replace the generation of Beecham, Toscanini, Koussevitzky and Sargent. And yet the sales of records proved that his hold over a broad section of the musical public remained remarkably strong. Sibelius's popularity thus seems likely to last, although it is based on a small number of his most accessible works, such as the Second Symphony and the Violin Concerto, rather than on his profoundest masterpieces, *Tapiola, Luonnotar, The*

Overleaf: 91, 92
The interior of Ainola.
93　Lighting a cigar.
94　From the balcony
of Ainola

◀ 89　Sir Thomas Beecham and Sibelius at Ainola, 1950s

95, 96 At the piano. Right, in the library

Bard and the Sixth Symphony. (Much the same can be said of Bartók or
Stravinsky; indeed, all the great masters have reached the broadest
public only through a handful of their works.)

Sibelius's acutely developed sense of identification with nature, and
his preoccupation with myth, constitute both a unique strength and a
profound limitation. For these preoccupations seem often to override
his involvement in the human condition, except in so far as man's relationship with nature is concerned. The regional flavour of much of
his art, the icy, northern intensity of his inspiration, often obscures its

97 Sibelius with his wife

inner warmth; and yet the sense of nature's power, which is the theme of *Tapiola* and the Seventh Symphony, is a universal, not a regional, experience. Few composers have shown themselves so remarkably equipped in their sense of form: one might even speak of Sibelius's capacity for 'continuous creation', so organically does his music grow. It was his good fortune to unite two traditions: that of the nineteenth-century tone-poem, with its national and programmatic overtones, and that of the classical symphony in its purest form. Whatever fluctuations his public reputation may undergo, this achievement stands.

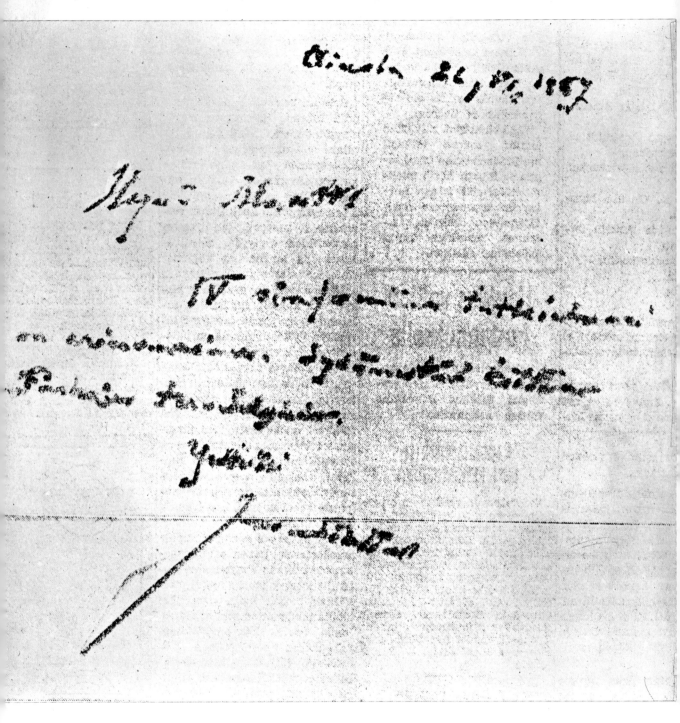

98   Sibelius's last letter to Martti Similä, written a couple of months before his death

99   Sibelius's tombstone at Ainola

CHRONOLOGY AND INDEX

1865 8 December, Sibelius born in Hämeenlinna.

1868 July, his father dies during cholera epidemic.

1875 First attempt at composition, *Vattendroppar (Drops of Water),* a little piece for violin and cello.

1876 Is enrolled at the *Hämeenlinna Suomalainen Normaalilyseo,* Finnish-speaking grammar school.

1880 Begins his studies of the violin with Gustav Levander.

1882 Composes a piano trio in A minor.

1885 Enters the Tsar Alexander University of Helsinki as a law student.

1886 Abandons law studies and devotes himself entirely to music.

1887 Plays in the quartet of the Helsinki School of Music and composes a good deal of chamber music.

1888 Meets Ferruccio Busoni, with whom he becomes firm friends.

1889 In the spring, a suite in A major and a string quartet are performed with success.
His studies in Helsinki completed, he proceeds to Berlin; here he begins work on the G minor piano quintet and meets Kajanus.

1890 Quartet in B flat, op. 4, performed. In the autumn, engagement to Aino Järnefelt.
Continues his studies abroad, this time in Vienna.

1891 Begins work on the 'Kullervo' Symphony.

1892 First performance and triumphant success of 'Kullervo'.
He composes *En Saga.*
June 10, marries Aino Järnefelt.
Appointed to teach in the School of Music.

1893 Composes the Karelia music, *The Swan of Tuonela* and a piano sonata.

1896 First performance of the 'Four Legends', and composition and first performance of *The Maiden in the Tower.*

1897 Award of an annual pension from the Finnish Government.

1898 Composes the *King Christian* suite (first performed in February) and visits Berlin.

1899 First Symphony completed and performed.

1900 Sibelius's music, including the new symphony, is the main attraction in tour made by Helsinki City Orchestra in northern Europe.

1901 Visits Rapallo and begins work on a new symphony.

1902 March 8, Second Symphony performed.

1903 Completes first version of the Violin Concerto.

1904 Moves to Järvenpää.
Begins Third Symphony.

1905 Second Symphony performed in Berlin and in Manchester.
Violin Concerto first performed under Richard Strauss.
Visits England.